PRIMA Official Game Guide
Written by Fernando Bueno
Prima Games
A Division of Random House, Inc.
www.primagames.com

Product Manager: Jason Wigle

Editor: Rebecca Chastain

Design: Graphic Applications Group, Inc.

Layout: Scott Watanabe

Fernando Bueno

Fernando "Red Star" Bueno has been a gamer since opening his first Atari, and has been writing creatively since his early years in high school. During college he combined his loves for gaming and writing and began freelancing for popular gaming websites.

The San Diego native found his way to Northern California shortly after high school. After graduating from the University of California, Davis, with a dual degree in English and art history, he was able to land a job as an editor for Prima Games. Though happy with his position as an editor, his life called him to Las Vegas where he now resides. During the move to Nevada, he also made the move to author and has since written a number of game books, including *50 Cent: Bulletproof, Prince of Persia: Two Thrones, AND 1,* and *Stubbs the Zombie*.

In his off time he enjoys the works of Hermann Hesse, Johann Van Goethe, Franz Kafka, Thomas Mann, and EGM. When not writing for Prima, he continues to perfect his craft as a poet.

We want to hear from you! E-mail comments and feedback to fbueno@primagames.com.

ISBN: 0-7615-5443-2

Library of Congress Catalog Card Number: 200693048

Printed in the United States of America

06 07 08 09 LL 10 9 8 7 6 5 4 3 2 1

NINETY-NINE NIGHTS, NINETY-NINE TALES

N3: Ninety-Nine Nights is an intricate tale involving nearly that many characters. Leaders of Light, Outlanders, and Dark Armies all have a stake in the outcome of the war between Humans and Goblins.

To see the full story behind *N3: Ninety-Nine Nights*, play through each character's missions. There will be twists, turns, and unexpected events throughout. The only way to get through them all is with this guide. To arms, valiant warrior!

USING THIS GUIDE

This guide is separated into seven different mini-guides, and each playable character has his or her own section detailing biographical background, statistics, weapons, combo attacks, and mission walkthrough. Simply flip to the character's main page and read on.

Throughout your journey, however, you will require additional information that applies to every character. Things such as general controls, items and power-ups, and information on unlockables are all detailed in their respective chapters. To access what you need, refer to the table of contents.

EMBARKING ON YOUR ADVENTURE

MAIN MENU

Main Menu

Character Select

Choose Start at the main screen to access the Main menu. Choose Select Character and decide on whose story you want to experience. Each character has his or her own story with slight variations on the tale, so be sure to experience all of them.

LOAD

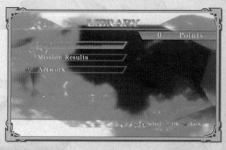

Select Load to play an existing file for any particular character. Be forewarned, however; you must save each character into an individual save file.

LIBRARY

The Library is where all unlocked content is stored. Character profiles, mission results, artwork, and more; it's all there. To access it

you must use points acquired by clearing missions—choose wisely, because there are no refunds.

OPTIONS

Choose Options to change the volume, camera orientation, vibration function, and contrast settings.

- **Music**—Adjusts the volume for the in-game music.
- **Sound Effects**—Adjusts the volume for the sound effects.
- **Voices**—Adjusts the volume for the dialogue.
- **Camera**—Changes either the up/down or left/right axis from normal to inverted.
- **Vibration**—Toggles the vibration function on or off.
- **Contrast**—Adjusts the contrast for better visibility.

N3 ナインティナイン・ナイツ NINETY-NINE NIGHTS

TUTORIAL

Play through the tutorial for hands-on practice with the control scheme. However, if ever you need a quick reference guide, look no further than the following pages.

TIPS, NOTES, AND CAUTIONS

TIP

These are bits of information that help you make better decisions. Pay attention; you might learn something.

NOTE

Note boxes provide general information that may not directly affect gameplay. At times, they might tell you more about the game or this guide.

CAUTION

Caution boxes always contain vital information. Usually they provide warnings of particular dangers and keep you alive.

BRANCHING TALE

Because *N3: Ninety-Nine Nights* is an intricate tale woven by the story threads of multiple characters, the plot may sometimes branch off in different directions. Refer to these boxes to help keep up.

CONTROLLING THE TIDES OF BATTLE

Though each character has a particular set of combo attacks, the control scheme is generally the same across all characters. Some have minor variations, but all respond to the same commands.

WALK AND RUN

Use the left analog stick to move about the battlefield. Press it in any given direction and your character will walk in that direction. Press lightly to walk cautiously; press it firmly and you will run.

NORMAL AND HEAVY ATTACKS

Engage the enemy in battle by pressing Ⓧ to execute a normal attack. To execute a heavy attack, press Ⓨ. Refer to the character combo lists to learn how to chain these two buttons into damaging attacks.

BLOCK AND DASH

Every now and again, the time comes when one must fight defensively. Blocking and dashing are both very useful in that respect.

To block, press ⒧. To dash, press ⒭. While blocking an attack leaves you in a stationary position, dashing is an effective means to get out of an attacker's range.

NOTE

Not all characters can execute the dash move. Tyurru, for example, executes a short evasive retreat when you press ⒭.

JUMP

Press Ⓐ to jump. Because the game doesn't have multi-tiered levels to traverse, jumping is usually a means to escape a group or begin an attack.

NOTE

As with dashing, not every character can jump. Klarrann's jump is replaced by an extremely useful stun move named Kneel Before Spirits.

ORB ATTACKS AND ORB SPARKS

Pressing Ⓑ activates either an Orb Attack (emptying your red Orb gauge) or an Orb Spark (emptying the blue gauge). An Orb Attack enhances your normal and heavy attacks and makes you significantly more powerful. Enemies that fall victim to an Orb Attack release blue Orbs.

Once the Orb Spark meter has filled with blue Orbs, you can unleash an Orb Spark attack. This move instantly kills all your enemies. Use both moves wisely.

NOTE

Once activated, each attack grants you momentary invincibility.

CONTROLLING YOUR TROOPS

You are not alone in battle. During most missions you have a choice between taking infantry, heavy infantry, pikemen, or archers into battle with you.

Assign one group to each bumper. The left squad is assigned to ⒃, while the right squad is assigned to ⒧. Press each bumper to activate or deactivate each squad. When the circle at a soldier's feet is solid, the soldier is active. If the circle is a dashed line, the soldier is inactive.

After assigning a squad to each bumper, you can order them about using the D-pad. Pressing up on the D-pad orders your troops on the offensive. Down on the D-pad sets them to a more cautious defensive stance.

Pay close attention to the bottom of your screen. The icons there tell you what class your squad is and if it is active or damaged. Reference the following table to see what each icon means.

Guard Icons

Icon	Meaning
	Troop health is at maximum.
	Troops have taken minor damage.
	Troops have taken moderate damage.
	Troops are in danger of being eliminated.
	Troops are in attack mode.
	Troops are in defense mode.
	Troops are either slain or inactive.
	Troops are infantry class.
	Troops are heavy infantry class.
	Troops are pikemen class.
	Troops are archer class.

SURVIVING
N3: NINETY-NINE NIGHTS

Before embarking on one of seven journeys, read this chapter to learn how to best approach a given situation. The strategies employed in the following pages can be useful no matter which character you choose.

COMBO RECOVERY

In the heat of battle it is easy to get carried away with your attacks. Though this sometimes kills multiple enemies at once, it can leave you in a very vulnerable position should you miss.

To avoid dangerous counterattacks, use controlled combo attacks. Quickly recover,

(should your sweeps miss) by dashing away. Not only do you minimize damage, but you also gain a distance advantage from which to launch another combo attack.

SITUATIONAL AWARENESS

The battlefield is a large area to keep track of. Enemies swarm behind you, amass in front of you, and even flank you. Instead of blindly launching yourself into battle, or even worse, forgetting your position on the field, use the camera to see everything around you.

During battle, swing the camera around to see where enemies approach from. The map indicators are useful in this same fashion, but only the camera gives you a real view of the distance between you and the enemy troops that approach from behind.

ELIMINATING ARCHERS

Archers are one of the most dangerous enemy groups. Because they are typically stationed away from the battle zone, they are usually out of harm's reach—your reach. If they go uncontested, they can stand there and pick apart you and your troops all day.

Luckily, they are also one of the enemy groups with the lowest HP value. Dispatch enemy archers quickly by simply rushing into them. When you are within close-combat range, they put away their bows and pull out their blades. Often, they just scatter and try to relocate, thus bringing an end to their barrage of arrows. Always approach the archers in a zigzag pattern to keep damage at a minimum.

FIGHT ON YOUR OWN TERMS

One of the worst things you can let happen on the battlefield is to let your enemies draw you into their kind of battle. If you play by their rules, you are at a handicap.

Always single out enemy bosses to make sure they are completely alone and have no help from their support squads. Similarly, when inside a large mass of enemy troops, run outside of the skirmish to draw them out. Once they give chase, they form a compact line of enemies behind you. When they do, turn around and strike them down.

A LITTLE HELP FROM YOUR FRIENDS

Just as you would not have an enemy boss fight with his troops by his side, you should always ensure that you do. This is war, not a friendly game of chess. Fight to win.

Preserve your troops at all costs. Sometimes you must venture ahead and draw out enemy traps so that your troops do not get ambushed. That way, your troops stay fresh and ready to fight.

WASTE NOT, WANT NOT

It may be tempting to snatch up an item as soon as it pops up on the field or, even worse, smash open a chest as soon as you see it. The prospect of topping off your health bar may seem too difficult to resist at times, but do!

Items may eventually fade away into nothingness, but wasting an item is much more detrimental than if you were to let one pass prematurely. Always use an item *only* when it will be of good use. Patience is a virtue.

ALWAYS BE PREPARED

There is a popular idiom that every combatant should keep in mind during battle: "Always be prepared."

At the beginning of every battle, take a moment to pause the game and rifle through your equipable items. Equip items to boost guard units or augment your own stat deficiencies. If at any point in mid-battle your units should fall, unequip the items that helped boost their stats.

NOTE

A comprehensive "Item Compendium" is at the end of this book. It details every item in the game with stat bonuses and other effects.

THE ENVIRONMENT IS YOUR FRIEND

Never lose sight of where you are fighting. Often, the area around you can be your best ally. Narrow passages, loose rocks, and even structures and cliff sides can be used to your advantage.

Draw large crowds into narrow paths to more easily attack their numbers or bully enemies against immovable objects like towers to keep them from escaping. When you need protection, dart behind towers, pillars, and around corners to save your hide.

BOWL OVER THE ENEMY

If an enemy can use boulders to flatten you like a pancake, then surely you can do the same. You will, at times, encounter boulders corralled by small wooden fences. When enemies approach from the base of a hill, attack the fence and let the boulders loose. They go barreling down on your foes, squashing them in the process.

Enemies killed by boulders also release red Orbs!

STRATEGIC STRIKES

War has a funny way of making you forget that your life is on the line. It is in those moments that you must stop, recollect, reassess, and re-approach a situation. An example of a good situation to do this in is when you see a large group of enemies amassed ahead of you. Your immediate reaction might be to charge at straight at them.

Instead, charge straight *through* them. Rush past enemies and emerge from the other side of their ranks. In doing so, you leave your troops trailing you and consequently on the opposite side of the large group. Turn around and you have the enemy pinched between you and your troops. This tactic is also effective on a smaller scale with enemy bosses. Pinch the boss between you and other generals to keep the boss on the defensive.

ENEMY PRIORITY

Watching battalions of enemies stroll onto the battlefield may be like watching a chef stock up a buffet; where do you start?

On the battlefield, wizards should be your first course. Attack wizards first, as they are capable of casting nasty spells that interrupt your attacks, slow you down, or turn your troops against you. Next should be archers. Break them up by lunging into their center and scattering their numbers.

LEVEL UP

Though not a practical solution to a difficult situation, repeating a previously accomplished mission for extra XP is not a bad idea.

Check your Orb XP meter in the Status screen to see how close you are to your next level, and consequently your next set of combo attacks, then check your Mission Results in the Library to see which missions yield the necessary number of Orbs to level up. Repeat missions to level up and you will not only gain the extra level, but you will also get more practice with your already-acquired combos. It's a win-win situation.

LIGHT AND DARK, CAPTAINS AND CATALYSTS

Every war has people that affect the outcome in little ways. This war is no different. Though each side has its own main players, not all characters affect the war as deeply.

WARRIORS OF THE LIGHT

Badokk

Badokk is leader of the mercenary division of the Temple Knights. He is responsible for recruiting and training mercenaries to aid in the war.

Category	Lvl. 1	Lvl. 2	Lvl. 3	Lvl. 4	Lvl. 5	Lvl. 6	Lvl. 7	Lvl. 8	Lvl. 9
Default Attack Point	150	165	182	200	220	242	266	292	322
Default HP	1,300	1,584	2,052	3,012	4,126	5,200	8,400	11,600	16,400
Default Defense Point	55	61	67	73	81	89	97	107	118
Default Rate of Critical Hit	5	6	7	8	9	10	11	12	13

Ectvarr

Ectvarr is the priestess of the Light. She alone controls the Orb of Light and is capable of granting its protection on whom she sees fit.

Epharr

Epharr is a mercenary with a mysterious past that haunts her. She is very passionate about warring with the Orcs. She fights alongside Myifee and the other mercenaries.

Category	Lvl. 1	Lvl. 2	Lvl. 3	Lvl. 4	Lvl. 5	Lvl. 6	Lvl. 7	Lvl. 8	Lvl. 9
Default Attack Point	130	143	157	173	190	209	230	253	279
Default HP	1,600	1,900	2,200	3,200	3,600	4,400	6,000	9,000	12,000
Default Defense Point	55	61	67	73	81	89	97	107	118
Default Rate of Critical Hit	5	6	7	8	9	10	11	12	13

The Family of Varrvazzar

You left Varrvazarr forever. There's no reason for you to return.

The family of Varrvazzar is strong and proud. Lord Vydenn and his three sons—Vyertenn, Vyarrhertenn, and Vyden—protect the lands from the invading hordes.

Lord Vydenn

Category	Lvl. 1	Lvl. 2	Lvl. 3	Lvl. 4	Lvl. 5	Lvl. 6	Lvl. 7	Lvl. 8	Lvl. 9
Default Attack Point	120	132	145	160	176	193	213	234	257
Default HP	1,700	2,210	2,612	3,122	3,622	4,222	5,084	6,209	6,830
Default Defense Point	55	61	67	73	81	89	97	107	118
Default Rate of Critical Hit	5	6	7	8	9	10	11	12	13

Vyarrhertenn

Category	Lvl. 1	Lvl. 2	Lvl. 3	Lvl. 4	Lvl. 5	Lvl. 6	Lvl. 7	Lvl. 8	Lvl. 9
Default Attack Point	120	132	145	160	176	193	213	234	257
Default HP	1,400	1,680	2,016	2,419	2,903	3,484	4,180	5,016	6,020
Default Defense Point	55	66	79	95	114	137	164	197	236
Default Rate of Critical Hit	0	0	0	0	0	0	0	0	0

Vyertenn

Category	Lvl. 1	Lvl. 2	Lvl. 3	Lvl. 4	Lvl. 5	Lvl. 6	Lvl. 7	Lvl. 8	Lvl. 9
Default Attack Point	120	132	145	160	176	193	213	234	257
Default HP	1,400	1,680	2,016	2,419	2,903	3,484	4,180	5,016	6,020
Default Defense Point	55	66	79	95	114	137	164	197	236
Default Rate of Critical Hit	0	0	0	0	0	0	0	0	0

Vyden

Category	Lvl. 1	Lvl. 2	Lvl. 3	Lvl. 4	Lvl. 5	Lvl. 6	Lvl. 7	Lvl. 8	Lvl. 9
Default Attack Point	120	132	145	160	176	193	213	234	257
Default HP	1,400	1,680	2,016	2,419	2,903	3,484	4,180	5,016	6,020
Default Defense Point	55	66	79	95	114	137	164	197	236
Default Rate of Critical Hit	0	0	0	0	0	0	0	0	0

Grorgann

Little is known about this general. He is loyal to the Temple Knights and aids Inphyy in her cause.

Category	Lvl. 1	Lvl. 2	Lvl. 3	Lvl. 4	Lvl. 5	Lvl. 6	Lvl. 7	Lvl. 8	Lvl. 9
Default Attack Point	150	161	172	184	197	210	225	241	258
Default HP	1,200	1,440	1,944	2,700	3,800	4,800	7,800	11,000	15,600
Default Defense Point	20	21	23	25	26	28	30	32	34
Default Rate of Critical Hit	5	6	7	8	9	10	11	12	13

Heppe

Heppe is one of Inphyy and Aspharr's generals. Young and eager to please, he plays a minor role in the life of the Temple Knight leaders.

Category	Lvl. 1	Lvl. 2	Lvl. 3	Lvl. 4	Lvl. 5	Lvl. 6	Lvl. 7	Lvl. 8	Lvl. 9
Default Attack Point	150	165	182	200	220	242	266	292	322
Default HP	1,200	1,440	1,944	2,700	3,800	4,800	7,800	11,000	15,600
Default Defense Point	55	61	67	73	81	89	97	107	118
Default Rate of Critical Hit	5	6	7	8	9	10	11	12	13

Tea Tea

Tea Tea is a misguided soul with a promising future. After encountering Myifee and his mercenary squad, Tea Tea joins in the war effort.

Category	Lvl. 1	Lvl. 2	Lvl. 3	Lvl. 4	Lvl. 5	Lvl. 6	Lvl. 7	Lvl. 8	Lvl. 9
Default Attack Point	130	143	157	173	190	209	230	253	279
Default HP	2,000	2,200	2,600	3,200	3,600	4,000	4,400	4,840	5,324
Default Defense Point	55	61	67	73	81	89	97	107	118
Default Rate of Critical Hit	5	6	7	8	9	10	11	12	13

MAGIC, MAYHEM, AND MYSTERY

Mylarrvaryss

Mylarrvaryss is a powerful wizard. He heads the sorcerer's academy that trained Tyurru and Yesperratt. His role in this war is to keep the balance between those who touch the Light and those who touch the Dark.

Category	Lvl. 1	Lvl. 2	Lvl. 3	Lvl. 4	Lvl. 5	Lvl. 6	Lvl. 7	Lvl. 8	Lvl. 9
Default Attack Point	170	187	206	226	249	274	301	331	364
Default HP	1,500	1,800	2,340	3,042	3,342	3,628	4,022	4,424	4,867
Default Defense Point	55	61	67	73	81	89	97	107	118
Default Rate of Critical Hit	5	6	7	8	9	10	11	12	13

Syumerrt

Syumerrt is a mysterious Elfin archer. He is good friends with Klarrann and a source of great knowledge.

Category	Lvl. 1	Lvl. 2	Lvl. 3	Lvl. 4	Lvl. 5	Lvl. 6	Lvl. 7	Lvl. 8	Lvl. 9
Default Attack Point	150	165	182	200	220	242	266	292	322
Default HP	2,000	2,200	2,600	4,000	4,600	5,200	5,600	6,600	13,222
Default Defense Point	55	61	67	73	81	89	97	107	118
Default Rate of Critical Hit	5	6	7	8	9	10	11	12	13

Yesperratt

Yesperratt is a young and powerful sorceress. She is also a dedicated soldier and follows Inphyy's orders without question.

Category	Lvl. 1	Lvl. 2	Lvl. 3	Lvl. 4	Lvl. 5	Lvl. 6	Lvl. 7	Lvl. 8	Lvl. 9
Default Attack Point	180	198	218	240	264	290	319	351	386
Default HP	1,700	2,040	2,448	2,938	3,525	4,230	5,076	6,091	7,310
Default Defense Point	55	66	79	95	114	137	164	197	236
Default Rate of Critical Hit	0	0	0	0	0	0	0	0	0

CATALYSTS FOR CHANGE

Dwinga

Dwinga is Dwingvatt's older brother. His death moves the otherwise shy Dwingvatt to join Dwykfarrio's army.

Dwinkle

This little Goblin is frightened of the war. His friendly nature leads him to form a bond with VigkVagk, the Troll, which then, in turn, influences the Troll's actions.

OUTLANDERS AND DARK WARRIORS

Chieftain Leuu

Chieftain Leuu, leader of the Orcs, is a nasty creature. He joins Dwykfarrio in the war against the Humans hoping to capitalize on the war by acquiring more Human slaves.

Category	Lvl. 1	Lvl. 2	Lvl. 3	Lvl. 4	Lvl. 5	Lvl. 6	Lvl. 7	Lvl. 8	Lvl. 9
Default Attack Point	170	187	206	226	249	274	301	331	364
Default HP	2,000	2,400	3,800	4,900	6,000	6,500	8,000	9,600	11,520
Default Defense Point	55	61	67	73	81	89	97	107	118
Default Rate of Critical Hit	10	11	12	13	14	15	16	17	18

Dwykfarrio

Dwykfarrio may have been a noble Goblin king once. Now he is possessed, seduced even, by the thought of acquiring both Orbs.

Category	Lvl. 1	Lvl. 2	Lvl. 3	Lvl. 4	Lvl. 5	Lvl. 6	Lvl. 7	Lvl. 8	Lvl. 9
Default Attack Point	170	197	229	265	308	357	414	480	557
Default HP	2,000	2,600	3,380	4,394	5,712	7,426	9,654	12,550	16,315
Default Defense Point	55	61	67	73	81	89	97	107	118
Default Rate of Critical Hit	10	11	12	13	14	15	16	17	18

King Gyagarr

King Gyagarr is leader of the Gewgs, a lizardlike race. Its warriors are fierce and unfriendly.

Category	Lvl. 1	Lvl. 2	Lvl. 3	Lvl. 4
Default Attack Point	800	1,200	1,800	2,700
Default HP	190	217	247	281
Default Defense Point	55	66	79	95
Default Rate of Critical Hit	0	5	15	15

King of Nights

This mysterious figure has a history shrouded in evil. Now he sits in the underworld, affecting the outcome of the world with his pawns.

Category	Lvl. 1	Lvl. 2	Lvl. 3	Lvl. 4	Lvl. 5	Lvl. 6	Lvl. 7	Lvl. 8	Lvl. 9
Default Attack Point	170	197	229	265	308	357	414	480	557
Default HP	2,000	3,000	4,500	6,750	10,125	15,188	22,781	34,172	51,258
Default Defense Point	90	108	130	156	187	224	269	322	387
Default Rate of Critical Hit	10	11	12	13	14	15	16	17	18

Ppakk the Third

Ppakk the Third is leader of the Pwuck army. This mischievous clan is quick to jump into action.

Category	Lvl. 1	Lvl. 2	Lvl. 3	Lvl. 4	Lvl. 5	Lvl. 6	Lvl. 7	Lvl. 8	Lvl. 9
Default Attack Point	180	207	238	274	315	362	416	479	551
Default HP	2,000	2,600	3,380	5,100	6,400	7,800	9,300	10,900	12,600
Default Defense Point	55	66	79	95	114	137	164	197	236
Default Rate of Critical Hit	10	11	12	13	14	15	16	17	18

Pyurrott

Pyurrott is an intriguing figure. She is chieftain of the Arphann, who control the dragon forces. Though she is often aligned with the Outlands tribes, she aids Klarrann and Syumerrt in finding the truth.

Category	Lvl. 1	Lvl. 2	Lvl. 3	Lvl. 4	Lvl. 5	Lvl. 6	Lvl. 7	Lvl. 8	Lvl. 9
Default Attack Point	180	207	238	274	315	362	416	479	551
Default HP	1,500	2,100	2,940	4,116	5,762	8,067	11,294	15,812	22,137
Default Defense Point	55	66	79	95	114	137	164	197	236
Default Rate of Critical Hit	10	11	12	13	14	15	16	17	18

GENERAL UNITS

Dark Elf Corporal

Category	Lvl. 1	Lvl. 2	Lvl. 3	Lvl. 4	Lvl. 5	Lvl. 6
Default Attack Point	140	161	185	213	245	282
Default HP	500	575	661	760	875	1,006
Default Defense Point	55	63	73	84	96	111
Default Rate of Critical Hit	0	0	0	0	0	0

Dark Elf Soldier

Category	Lvl. 1	Lvl. 2	Lvl. 3	Lvl. 4	Lvl. 5	Lvl. 6
Default Attack Point	100	115	132	152	175	201
Default HP	180	207	238	274	315	362
Default Defense Point	55	63	73	84	96	111
Default Rate of Critical Hit	0	0	0	0	0	0

Dragon

Category	Lvl. 1	Lvl. 2	Lvl. 3	Lvl. 4
Default Attack Point	80	88	97	106
Default HP	70	77	85	93
Default Defense Point	55	61	67	73
Default Rate of Critical Hit	0	5	15	15

Goblin Archer

Category	Lvl. 1	Lvl. 2	Lvl. 3	Lvl. 4	Lvl. 5	Lvl. 6	Lvl. 7	Lvl. 8
Default Attack Point	70	77	85	93	102	113	124	136
Default HP	140	154	169	186	205	225	248	273
Default Defense Point	55	61	67	73	81	89	97	107
Default Rate of Critical Hit	0	5	15	15	20	25	25	30

Goblin Catapult

Category	Lvl. 1	Lvl. 2	Lvl. 3	Lvl. 4
Default Attack Point	220	220	220	220
Default HP	2,200	2,200	2,200	2,200
Default Defense Point	35	39	42	47
Default Rate of Critical Hit	0	0	10	10

Goblin Catapult Engineer 1

Category	Lvl. 1	Lvl. 2	Lvl. 3	Lvl. 4	Lvl. 5	Lvl. 6	Lvl. 7	Lvl. 8
Default Attack Point	90	99	109	120	132	145	159	175
Default HP	450	495	545	599	659	725	797	877
Default Defense Point	55	61	67	73	81	89	97	107
Default Rate of Critical Hit	0	0	10	10	20	20	20	25

Goblin Catapult Engineer 2

Category	Lvl. 1	Lvl. 2	Lvl. 3	Lvl. 4	Lvl. 5	Lvl. 6	Lvl. 7	Lvl. 8
Default Attack Point	90	99	109	120	132	145	159	175
Default HP	1,000	1,100	1,210	1,331	1,464	1,611	1,772	1,949
Default Defense Point	55	61	67	73	81	89	97	107
Default Rate of Critical Hit	0	0	10	10	20	20	20	25

Elf Soldier

Category	Lvl. 1	Lvl. 2	Lvl. 3	Lvl. 4
Default Attack Point	170	190	213	239
Default HP	1,000	1,200	1,440	1,728
Default Defense Point	55	66	79	95
Default Rate of Critical Hit	0	5	15	15

Gewg Corporal

Category	Lvl. 1	Lvl. 2	Lvl. 3	Lvl. 4
Default Attack Point	160	181	204	231
Default HP	650	780	936	1,123
Default Defense Point	55	66	79	95
Default Rate of Critical Hit	0	5	15	15

Gewg Soldier

Category	Lvl. 1	Lvl. 2	Lvl. 3	Lvl. 4
Default Attack Point	140	158	179	202
Default HP	400	480	576	691
Default Defense Point	55	66	79	95
Default Rate of Critical Hit	0	5	15	15

Goblin Commanding Officer

Category	Lvl. 1	Lvl. 2	Lvl. 3	Lvl. 4	Lvl. 5	Lvl. 6	Lvl. 7	Lvl. 8
Default Attack Point	150	165	182	200	220	242	266	292
Default HP	1,000	1,300	1,690	2,197	2,856	3,713	4,827	6,275
Default Defense Point	55	61	67	73	81	89	97	107
Default Rate of Critical Hit	10	11	12	13	14	15	16	17

Goblin Elite Archer

Category	Lvl. 1	Lvl. 2	Lvl. 3	Lvl. 4	Lvl. 5	Lvl. 6	Lvl. 7	Lvl. 8
Default Attack Point	90	99	109	120	132	145	159	175
Default HP	210	231	254	280	307	338	372	409
Default Defense Point	55	61	67	73	81	89	97	107
Default Rate of Critical Hit	0	5	15	15	20	25	25	30

Goblin Elite Soldier (One-Handed Sword)

Category	Lvl. 1	Lvl. 2	Lvl. 3	Lvl. 4	Lvl. 5	Lvl. 6	Lvl. 7	Lvl. 8
Default Attack Point	90	99	109	120	132	145	159	175
Default HP	270	297	327	359	395	435	478	526
Default Defense Point	55	61	67	73	81	89	97	107
Default Rate of Critical Hit	0	0	10	10	20	20	20	25

Goblin Elite Soldier (Spear)

Category	Lvl. 1	Lvl. 2	Lvl. 3	Lvl. 4	Lvl. 5	Lvl. 6	Lvl. 7	Lvl. 8
Default Attack Point	110	121	133	146	161	177	195	214
Default HP	280	308	339	373	410	451	496	546
Default Defense Point	55	61	67	73	81	89	97	107
Default Rate of Critical Hit	0	5	15	15	20	25	25	30

Goblin Soldier (One-Handed Sword)

Category	Lvl. 1	Lvl. 2	Lvl. 3	Lvl. 4	Lvl. 5	Lvl. 6	Lvl. 7	Lvl. 8
Default Attack Point	70	77	85	93	102	113	124	136
Default HP	170	187	206	226	249	274	301	331
Default Defense Point	55	61	67	73	81	89	97	107
Default Rate of Critical Hit	0	0	10	10	20	20	20	25

Goblin Soldier (Spear)

Category	Lvl. 1	Lvl. 2	Lvl. 3	Lvl. 4	Lvl. 5	Lvl. 6	Lvl. 7	Lvl. 8
Default Attack Point	70	77	85	93	102	113	124	136
Default HP	190	209	230	253	278	306	337	370
Default Defense Point	55	61	67	73	81	89	97	107
Default Rate of Critical Hit	0	5	15	15	20	25	25	30

Goblin Wizard

Category	Lvl. 1	Lvl. 2	Lvl. 3	Lvl. 4
Default Attack Point	180	212	251	296
Default HP	750	900	1,080	1,296
Default Defense Point	55	66	79	95
Default Rate of Critical Hit	0	0	0	0

Mercenary (One-Handed Sword)

Category	Lvl. 1	Lvl. 2	Lvl. 3	Lvl. 4	Lvl. 5	Lvl. 6	Lvl. 7	Lvl. 8
Default Attack Point	70	77	85	93	102	113	124	136
Default HP	350	385	424	466	512	564	620	682
Default Defense Point	55	61	67	73	81	89	97	107
Default Rate of Critical Hit	0	5	15	15	20	25	25	30

Mercenary (Two-Handed Sword)

Category	Lvl. 1	Lvl. 2	Lvl. 3	Lvl. 4	Lvl. 5	Lvl. 6	Lvl. 7	Lvl. 8
Default Attack Point	80	88	97	106	117	129	142	156
Default HP	350	385	424	466	512	564	620	682
Default Defense Point	55	61	67	73	81	89	97	107
Default Rate of Critical Hit	0	5	15	15	20	25	25	30

Ninety-Nine Nights Forces

Category	Lvl. 1	Lvl. 2	Lvl. 3	Lvl. 4
Default Attack Point	200	236	278	329
Default HP	500	625	781	977
Default Defense Point	55	66	79	95
Default Rate of Critical Hit	0	0	0	0

Orc Commanding Officer

Category	Lvl. 1	Lvl. 2	Lvl. 3	Lvl. 4	Lvl. 5	Lvl. 6	Lvl. 7	Lvl. 8	Lvl. 9	Lvl. 10	Lvl. 11
Default Attack Point	160	176	194	213	234	258	283	312	343	377	415
Default HP	1,200	1,560	2,028	2,636	3,427	4,456	5,792	7,530	9,789	12,725	16,543
Default Defense Point	55	61	67	73	81	89	97	107	118	130	143
Default Rate of Critical Hit	10	11	12	13	14	15	16	17	18	25	25

Orc Elite Commanding Officer

Category	Lvl. 1	Lvl. 2	Lvl. 3	Lvl. 4	Lvl. 5	Lvl. 6	Lvl. 7	Lvl. 8	Lvl. 9	Lvl. 10	Lvl. 11
Default Attack Point	170	187	206	226	249	274	301	331	364	401	441
Default HP	1,200	1,560	2,028	2,636	3,427	4,456	5,792	7,530	9,789	12,725	16,543
Default Defense Point	55	61	67	73	81	89	97	107	118	130	143
Default Rate of Critical Hit	10	11	12	13	14	15	16	17	18	25	25

Orc Elite Corporal (Heavy Spear)

Category	Lvl. 1	Lvl. 2	Lvl. 3	Lvl. 4	Lvl. 5	Lvl. 6	Lvl. 7	Lvl. 8	Lvl. 9	Lvl. 10	Lvl. 11
Default Attack Point	170	182	195	208	223	238	255	273	292	313	334
Default HP	1,000	1,070	1,145	1,225	1,311	1,403	1,501	1,606	1,718	1,838	1,967
Default Defense Point	55	59	63	67	72	77	83	88	95	101	108
Default Rate of Critical Hit	0	0	10	10	20	20	20	20	25	25	25

Orc Elite Corporal (Light Spear)

Category	Lvl. 1	Lvl. 2	Lvl. 3	Lvl. 4	Lvl. 5	Lvl. 6	Lvl. 7	Lvl. 8	Lvl. 9	Lvl. 10	Lvl. 11
Default Attack Point	160	171	183	196	210	224	240	257	275	294	315
Default HP	1,000	1,070	1,145	1,225	1,311	1,403	1,501	1,606	1,718	1,838	1,967
Default Defense Point	55	59	63	67	72	77	83	88	95	101	108
Default Rate of Critical Hit	0	0	10	10	20	20	20	20	25	25	25

Orc Elite Soldier (Heavy Spear)

Category	Lvl. 1	Lvl. 2	Lvl. 3	Lvl. 4	Lvl. 5	Lvl. 6	Lvl. 7	Lvl. 8	Lvl. 9	Lvl. 10	Lvl. 11
Default Attack Point	140	150	160	172	184	196	210	225	241	257	275
Default HP	380	407	435	466	498	533	570	610	653	699	748
Default Defense Point	55	59	63	67	72	77	83	88	95	101	108
Default Rate of Critical Hit	0	0	10	10	20	20	20	20	25	25	25

Orc Elite Soldier (Light Spear)

Category	Lvl. 1	Lvl. 2	Lvl. 3	Lvl. 4	Lvl. 5	Lvl. 6	Lvl. 7	Lvl. 8	Lvl. 9	Lvl. 10	Lvl. 11
Default Attack Point	130	139	149	159	170	182	195	209	223	239	256
Default HP	380	407	435	466	498	533	570	610	653	699	748
Default Defense Point	55	59	63	67	72	77	83	88	95	101	108
Default Rate of Critical Hit	0	0	10	10	20	20	20	20	25	25	25

Orc Heavy-Armored Corporal (Heavy Spear)

Category	Lvl. 1	Lvl. 2	Lvl. 3	Lvl. 4	Lvl. 5	Lvl. 6	Lvl. 7	Lvl. 8	Lvl. 9	Lvl. 10	Lvl. 11
Default Attack Point	150	161	172	184	197	210	225	241	258	276	295
Default HP	760	813	870	931	996	1,066	1,141	1,220	1,306	1,397	1,495
Default Defense Point	55	59	63	67	72	77	83	88	95	101	108
Default Rate of Critical Hit	0	0	10	10	20	20	20	20	25	25	25

Orc Heavy-Armored Corporal (Light Spear)

Category	Lvl. 1	Lvl. 2	Lvl. 3	Lvl. 4	Lvl. 5	Lvl. 6	Lvl. 7	Lvl. 8	Lvl. 9	Lvl. 10	Lvl. 11
Default Attack Point	140	150	160	172	184	196	210	225	241	257	275
Default HP	760	813	870	931	996	1,066	1,141	1,220	1,306	1,397	1,495
Default Defense Point	55	59	63	67	72	77	83	88	95	101	108
Default Rate of Critical Hit	0	0	10	10	20	20	20	20	25	25	25

Orc Heavy-Armored Soldier (Heavy Spear)

Category	Lvl. 1	Lvl. 2	Lvl. 3	Lvl. 4	Lvl. 5	Lvl. 6	Lvl. 7	Lvl. 8	Lvl. 9	Lvl. 10	Lvl. 11
Default Attack Point	100	107	114	123	131	140	150	161	172	184	197
Default HP	180	193	206	221	236	252	270	289	309	331	354
Default Defense Point	55	59	63	67	72	77	83	88	95	101	108
Default Rate of Critical Hit	0	0	10	10	20	20	20	20	25	25	25

Orc Heavy-Armored Soldier (Light Spear)

Category	Lvl. 1	Lvl. 2	Lvl. 3	Lvl. 4	Lvl. 5	Lvl. 6	Lvl. 7	Lvl. 8	Lvl. 9	Lvl. 10	Lvl. 11
Default Attack Point	100	107	114	123	131	140	150	161	172	184	197
Default HP	180	193	206	221	236	252	270	289	309	331	354
Default Defense Point	55	59	63	67	72	77	83	88	95	101	108
Default Rate of Critical Hit	0	0	10	10	20	20	20	20	25	25	25

Orc Light-Armored Corporal (Heavy Spear)

Category	Lvl. 1	Lvl. 2	Lvl. 3	Lvl. 4	Lvl. 5	Lvl. 6	Lvl. 7	Lvl. 8	Lvl. 9	Lvl. 10	Lvl. 11
Default Attack Point	100	107	114	123	131	140	150	161	172	184	197
Default HP	500	535	572	613	655	701	750	803	859	919	984
Default Defense Point	55	59	63	67	72	77	83	88	95	101	108
Default Rate of Critical Hit	0	0	10	10	20	20	20	20	25	25	25

Orc Light-Armored Corporal (Light Spear)

Category	Lvl. 1	Lvl. 2	Lvl. 3	Lvl. 4	Lvl. 5	Lvl. 6	Lvl. 7	Lvl. 8	Lvl. 9	Lvl. 10	Lvl. 11
Default Attack Point	100	107	114	123	131	140	150	161	172	184	197
Default HP	500	535	572	613	655	701	750	803	859	919	984
Default Defense Point	55	59	63	67	72	77	83	88	95	101	108
Default Rate of Critical Hit	0	0	10	10	20	20	20	20	25	25	25

Orc Light-Armored Soldier (Heavy Spear)

Category	Lvl. 1	Lvl. 2	Lvl. 3	Lvl. 4	Lvl. 5	Lvl. 6	Lvl. 7	Lvl. 8	Lvl. 9	Lvl. 10	Lvl. 11
Default Attack Point	70	75	80	86	92	98	105	112	120	129	138
Default HP	140	150	160	172	184	196	210	225	241	257	275
Default Defense Point	55	59	63	67	72	77	83	88	95	101	108
Default Rate of Critical Hit	0	0	10	10	20	20	20	20	25	25	25

Orc Light-Armored Soldier (Light Spear)

Category	Lvl. 1	Lvl. 2	Lvl. 3	Lvl. 4	Lvl. 5	Lvl. 6	Lvl. 7	Lvl. 8	Lvl. 9	Lvl. 10	Lvl. 11
Default Attack Point	80	86	92	98	105	112	120	128	137	147	157
Default HP	140	150	160	172	184	196	210	225	241	257	275
Default Defense Point	55	59	63	67	72	77	83	88	95	101	108
Default Rate of Critical Hit	0	0	10	10	20	20	20	20	25	25	25

Pwuck Corporal

Category	Lvl. 1	Lvl. 2	Lvl. 3	Lvl. 4
Default Attack Point	160	192	230	276
Default HP	650	780	936	1,123
Default Defense Point	55	66	79	95
Default Rate of Critical Hit	0	0	10	10

Pwuck Soldier

Category	Lvl. 1	Lvl. 2	Lvl. 3	Lvl. 4
Default Attack Point	120	144	173	207
Default HP	400	480	576	691
Default Defense Point	55	66	79	95
Default Rate of Critical Hit	0	0	10	10

Temple Knights Archer

Category	Lvl. 1	Lvl. 2	Lvl. 3	Lvl. 4	Lvl. 5	Lvl. 6	Lvl. 7	Lvl. 8
Default Attack Point	70	77	85	93	102	113	124	136
Default HP	220	242	266	293	322	354	390	429
Default Defense Point	55	61	67	73	81	89	97	107
Default Rate of Critical Hit	0	0	5	5	5	10	10	15

Temple Knights Commanding Officer (One-Handed Sword)

Category	Lvl. 1	Lvl. 2	Lvl. 3	Lvl. 4	Lvl. 5	Lvl. 6	Lvl. 7	Lvl. 8
Default Attack Point	120	132	145	160	176	193	213	234
Default HP	900	990	1,089	1,198	1,318	1,449	1,594	1,754
Default Defense Point55	61	67	73	81	89	97	107	
Default Rate of Critical Hit	0	5	5	10	10	10	15	20

Temple Knights Commanding Officer (Spear)

Category	Lvl. 1	Lvl. 2	Lvl. 3	Lvl. 4	Lvl. 5	Lvl. 6	Lvl. 7	Lvl. 8
Default Attack Point	120	132	145	160	176	193	213	234
Default HP	900	990	1,089	1,198	1,318	1,449	1,594	1,754
Default Defense Point	55	61	67	73	81	89	97	107
Default Rate of Critical Hit	0	5	5	10	10	10	15	20

Temple Knights Commanding Officer (Two-Handed Sword)

Category	Lvl. 1	Lvl. 2	Lvl. 3	Lvl. 4	Lvl. 5	Lvl. 6	Lvl. 7	Lvl. 8
Default Attack Point	120	132	145	160	176	193	213	234
Default HP	900	990	1,089	1,198	1,318	1,449	1,594	1,754
Default Defense Point	55	61	67	73	81	89	97	107
Default Rate of Critical Hit	0	5	5	10	10	10	15	20

Temple Knights Corporal (One-Handed Sword)

Category	Lvl. 1	Lvl. 2	Lvl. 3	Lvl. 4	Lvl. 5	Lvl. 6	Lvl. 7	Lvl. 8
Default Attack Point	90	99	109	120	132	145	159	175
Default HP	450	495	545	599	659	725	797	877
Default Defense Point	55	61	67	73	81	89	97	107
Default Rate of Critical Hit	0	5	5	10	10	10	15	20

Temple Knights Corporal (Spear)

Category	Lvl. 1	Lvl. 2	Lvl. 3	Lvl. 4	Lvl. 5	Lvl. 6	Lvl. 7	Lvl. 8
Default Attack Point	90	99	109	120	132	145	159	175
Default HP	450	495	545	599	659	725	797	877
Default Defense Point	55	61	67	73	81	89	97	107
Default Rate of Critical Hit	0	5	5	10	10	10	15	20

Temple Knights Corporal (Two-Handed Sword)

Category	Lvl. 1	Lvl. 2	Lvl. 3	Lvl. 4	Lvl. 5	Lvl. 6	Lvl. 7	Lvl. 8
Default Attack Point	90	99	109	120	132	145	159	175
Default HP	420	462	508	559	615	676	744	818
Default Defense Point	55	61	67	73	81	89	97	107
Default Rate of Critical Hit	0	5	5	10	10	10	15	20

Temple Knights Soldier (One-Handed Sword)

Category	Lvl. 1	Lvl. 2	Lvl. 3	Lvl. 4	Lvl. 5	Lvl. 6	Lvl. 7	Lvl. 8
Default Attack Point	70	77	85	93	102	113	124	136
Default HP	300	330	363	399	439	483	531	585
Default Defense Point	55	61	67	73	81	89	97	107
Default Rate of Critical Hit	0	0	5	5	5	10	10	15

Temple Knights Soldier (Spear)

Category	Lvl. 1	Lvl. 2	Lvl. 3	Lvl. 4	Lvl. 5	Lvl. 6	Lvl. 7	Lvl. 8
Default Attack Point	70	77	85	93	102	113	124	136
Default HP	290	319	351	386	425	467	514	565
Default Defense Point	55	61	67	73	81	89	97	107
Default Rate of Critical Hit	0	0	5	5	5	10	10	15

Temple Knights Soldier (Two-Handed Sword)

Category	Lvl. 1	Lvl. 2	Lvl. 3	Lvl. 4	Lvl. 5	Lvl. 6	Lvl. 7	Lvl. 8
Default Attack Point	70	77	85	93	102	113	124	136
Default HP	300	330	363	399	439	483	531	585
Default Defense Point	55	61	67	73	81	89	97	107
Default Rate of Critical Hit	0	0	5	5	5	10	10	15

Troll

Category	Lvl. 1	Lvl. 2	Lvl. 3	Lvl. 4
Default Attack Point	80	96	115	138
Default HP	900	1,080	1,296	1,555
Default Defense Point	55	66	79	95
Default Rate of Critical Hit	10	11	12	13

INPHYY'S ADVENTURE

Age:
17

Class:
Knight

Weapon:
Sword

Orb Spark:
Light

Inphyy is the daughter of a valiant warrior killed by Goblins. She trains rigorously as a knight and seeks revenge. Together with her brother Aspharr she leads the Temple Knights.

Trained to be a knight since youth, she is young and has an aura of something greater. Her bravado is often a way she hides her adoration for her older brother, Aspharr. She values the knightly code: justice and loyalty.

VITAL STATISTICS

Category	Level 1	Level 2	Level 3	Level 4	Level 5	Level 6	Level 7	Level 8	Level 9
Default Attack Point	100	110	121	133	146	161	177	195	214
Default HP	1,200	1,530	2,074	3,332	4,600	5,500	8,800	14,266	22,006
Default Defense Point	20	22	24	27	29	32	35	39	43
Default Rate of Critical Hit	11	12	13	14	15	16	17	18	19

COMBO ATTACKS

Inphyy's combo attacks are extremely dangerous. Her large, powerful swords can quickly inflict massive damage on multiple enemies. Her attacks tend to be wide-sweeping sword swings of furious anger.

Level 1

The table lists Inphyy's first set of devastating attacks. At level 1 she can execute a number of high-damage combos. As she levels up and learns more combos, these remain the base of her awesome fighting style.

NOTE

When doing a combo attack, execute button presses separated by commas in quick succession.

If the move says ", then" or ", press", allow the final move to finish before pressing the next button command.

Move	Execution
Bloody Storm	In mid-jump, press ⊗,⊗
Crimson Impact	During Orb Attack, press ⊗
Crimson Nova	During Orb Attack, press ⓨ
Dancing Sword	ⓨ,ⓨ,ⓨ
Double Fang	⊗,⊗,ⓨ,ⓨ
Mistral Attack	⊗,⊗,⊗,⊗
Red Break	ⓨ,ⓨ,ⓨ,⊗,⊗
Red Rising	In mid-jump, press ⓨ
Rising Slash	ⓡⓑ, then press ⊗
Stamping	Ⓐ
Stamping Dance	During headstomp, press ⓨ
Stamping Needle	During headstomp, press ⊗
Sword Slash	ⓨ,⊗
Wing Ring	⊗,ⓨ

TIP

To do a headstomp, execute a Stamping maneuver at an enemy. After pressing Ⓐ to jump, aim at and land on your target's head. Voilà—headstomp!

Level 2

Most of these combos add strikes to Inphyy's level 1 maneuvers. Though they simply add more swings of the sword, they elongate the combo chain, making it possible to create more havoc on the battlefield. Just as many of these combos' names suggest, the end result is bloody.

Move	Execution
Air Blade	In mid-jump, press ⊗ and then ⓨ
Bloody Rose	⊗,ⓨ,ⓨ
Bloody Sword	⊗,⊗,⊗,ⓨ
Bloody Moon	⊗,⊗,⊗,ⓨ,ⓨ
Crimson Moon	In mid-jump, press ⊗,⊗,⊗,⊗
Dancing Sword	ⓨ,ⓨ,ⓨ,ⓨ
Impact Attack	ⓨ,ⓨ,⊗
Impact Slash	While stabbing an enemy, press ⊗
Scarlet Break	ⓨ,ⓨ,ⓨ,⊗,ⓨ,⊗

TIP

To stab an enemy, execute Impact Attack.

Level 3

Inphyy's level 3 combos aren't many, but what they lack in number, they make up for in damage output. Moves like Mistral Attack and Crimson Break effectively destroy large clusters of enemies, while finishing moves like Impact Break are subtle reminders of Inphyy's inner rage.

Move	Execution
Crimson Break	ⓨ,ⓨ,ⓨ,⊗,⊗,⊗,⊗
Fang Slash	⊗,⊗,ⓨ,ⓨ,ⓨ
Impact Break	While stabbing an enemy, press ⓨ
Mistral Attack	⊗,⊗,⊗,⊗,⊗
Rising Break	ⓡⓑ, then press ⓨ

Level 4

At level 4, Inphyy learns a few new combo attacks. Most notable are Bloody Slash and High Jump. Both will be essential to her fighting arsenal.

Move	Execution
Bloody Cyclone	In mid-double jump, press ⊗
Bloody Slash	ⓨ,ⓨ,ⓨ,⊗,⊗,⊗,ⓨ (drains Orb Attack gauge)
High Jump	In mid-jump, press Ⓐ
Needle Slash	⊗,ⓨ,⊗
Red Rising	In mid-double jump, press ⓨ
Ring Fang	⊗,⊗,ⓨ,ⓨ,⊗
Scarlet Spiral	⊗,⊗,⊗,ⓨ,⊗
Scarlet Symphony	⊗,⊗,⊗,ⓨ,ⓨ
Vermillion Moon	In mid-jump, press ⊗,⊗,⊗,⊗,⊗

Level 5

Scarlet Prelude and Vermillion Full Moon join the high-damage-output combo list. Both are excellent ways to lay waste to a small group of enemies as they crowd around. Use Vermillion Full Moon to rain down death when they least expect it.

Move	Execution
Scarlet Prelude	X,X,X,Y,Y,Y
Vermillion Full Moon	In mid-jump, press X,X,X,X,X,X

Level 6

Inphyy is no stranger to doing combat from on high. Her wings may be decorative, but her leaping abilities are nothing less than deadly. Level 6 introduces another vicious combo attack from mid-jump; the Fly Highland may look like Vermillion Full Moon, but rest assured this one is deadlier.

Move	Execution
Fly Highland	In mid-jump, press X,X,X,X
Mistral Slash	X,X,X,X,X,X,X
Scarlet Finale	X,X,X,Y,Y,X

Level 7

As Inphyy nears the pinnacle of her fighting expertise, a few combo attacks from previous levels are enhanced. The Mistral and Scarlet series of maneuvers gain one more power-up before Inphyy tops off.

Move	Execution
Mistral Rush	X,X,X,X,X,X,X,X
Scarlet Nova	X,X,X,Y,X (drains Orb Attack gauge)

Level 8

At level 8, Inphyy acquires two of her most powerful attacks aside from the Orb Spark. Mistral Rush gets its final attack in the devastating combo chain, making it Inphyy's longest chain attack. Use it often and her enemies won't have a chance to retaliate before they meet their demise.

Move	Execution
Bright of Bright	Y,Y,Y,X,X,X,Y,X (drains Orb Attack gauge)
Mistral Rush	X,X,X,X,X,X,X,X

Level 9

Finally, the pinnacle of Inphyy's prowess. At level 9 Inphyy learns her final attack, Seraph Butterfly. This awesome move sends Inphyy swooping down on her enemy in a powerful rush from above.

Move	Execution
Seraph Butterfly	In mid-jump, press A,Y (drains Orb Attack gauge)

WEAPONS

Inphyy is very capable with steel. Her weapon of choice is the sword, and in her hands it becomes an extension of her body.

Temple Sword

Level 1

This sword is carried only by Temple Knights. It is Inphyy's default sword.

Klausorus

Level 1

An evil sword with the flames of destruction sealed within, Klausorus boosts Attack power 50 percent, Attack range 50 percent, and Orb Attack length 30 percent.

Bloody Rose

Level 2

The blade of this sword glistens in deep crimson, the color of blood. It adds 15 percent to Attack range.

Blaze Sword

Level 3

This is a sword the color of a blazing inferno. Attack power increases by 10 percent, Attack range by 20 percent, and critical rate by 10 percent.

TIP

To acquire Blaze Sword, play the tutorial before beginning a profile with Inphyy.

Orb Sword

Level 3

A divine sword that holds the power of the Orb within, the Orb Sword enhances Attack range by 25 percent and Orb appear rate by 15 percent.

Phoenix Blade

Level 4

A precious sword carved with the image of a phoenix, this weapon increases Attack range by 30 percent, Attack power by 20 percent, Defense power by 10 percent, and Orb Attack length by 10 percent.

Amethyst Saber

Level 6

Decorated with a bewitching amethyst crystal, this sword increases Attack range by 40 percent, critical rate by 50 percent, and Orb appear rate by 10 percent.

Prominence

Level 7

Prominence is a legendary sword from the netherworld. Attack range increases 50 percent, critical rate increases 30 percent, and Orb gauge charge speed also increases 30 percent when this sword is equipped. Trample Attack power also doubles.

Weapon Locations and Conditions

Weapon	Location/Condition
Temple Sword	Default weapon
Klausorus	Clear Eaurvarria Mountains with S Rank or dropped in Another World Mission
Bloody Rose	Treasure chest at the beginning of Eaurvarria Mountains
Blaze Sword	Treasure chest near the Eaurvarria Boss or treasure chest in Tutorial
Orb Sword	Treasure chest in Wyandeek Mission
Phoenix Blade	Treasure chest in Wyandeek Mission
Amethyst Saber	Treasure chest in Ywa-Ue-Uar Forest Mission
Prominence	Clear Pholya with A Rank

THE QUEST FOR VENGEANCE

Inphyy's mission to rid the world of the Goblins is a personal one. Though her brother fights to bring peace back to the world, her motives are much darker. Inphyy seeks vengeance for her father's death at Goblin hands.

DIVINE VARRFARRINN

Treasure Chest

Two have come forward as candidates to be the next leader of the Temple Knights: Aspharr, prudent and well respected, and Inphyy, remarkably developed as a knight through natural-born talent and sheer tenacity. One duel will determine who the next leader will be.

Your first task in asserting yourself as the Temple Knights' leader is to defeat 50 enemies. Luckily, the battlefield is rife with enemy grunts. Dash forward and let the cold steel in your hand warm itself with enemy blood.

Use small, sweeping combo attacks to fell enemies as you wend your way up the battlefield. The number of fallen enemies increases quickly, so don't hesitate to wade into an enemy squad with your blade leading the way.

OBJECTIVE
Defeat the enemy archers.

With 50 notches on your belt, enemy archers come into view in the near distance. Their arrows pose a great peril to your troops, and it is up to you to eliminate the threat.

Carefully clear a path up the nearby hillock where the enemy archers perch, and greet them with your blade. Zigzag toward them to keep their aim shifting, and sweep them with your blade as soon as you are within range.

After destroying the first archer squad, proceed to the second blip on your map highlighted in yellow. A second group of enemy archers awaits on another nearby hillock. Approach from a flank and dice them to bits.

As you do, you are met by General Grorgann. Welcome him to the battle by bashing his brains with your blade. Should you have a full Orb gauge, use it now to finish off the archers and whittle down Grorgann's health. If not,

make sure that Grorgann is square in the middle of your attacks as you diminish the archer ranks.

Grorgann falls to your blade, but the battle is far from over. Another enemy general joins the fray; Aspharr, your brother, comes dashing down the hillside with his spear ready at his side.

Block Aspharr's attacks and counterattack immediately. Strike with well-placed combos like the Mistral Attack, and knock him to the ground. As he lies on his back, fight off any encroaching enemies. As soon as he is back on his feet, resume your relentless fury and strike him down.

Caught up in the heat of the battle, you forget that this is only a test to see who should lead the Temple Knights. You swing your blade furiously at Aspharr as he nervously pleads for you to halt.

When you do, you stand the victor. During your knighting ceremony you, Aspharr, and the other generals are bestowed with the protection of the Light. With the power of good as your personal protector, how can anyone stand in the way of your holy mission?

EAURVARRIA MOUNTAINS

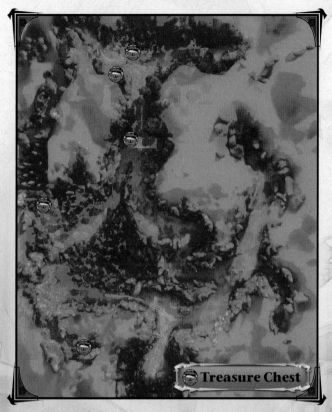

 **Treasure Chest**

In a duel to become leader of the Temple Knights, Inphyy leads the knights to the Eaurvarria Mountains, only to find a massive Goblin force marching for Varrfarrinn.

GUARD UNITS
Infantry
Archers

OBJECTIVE
Destroy the enemy.

Be not afraid to meet the Goblin horde head on. Leave your guard units behind at first to maximize your combo potential. After all, the fewer enemies your guards eliminate, the more enemies you can add to combo chain.

Head blade-first into the middle of the approaching Goblin horde, and swing angrily once they engulf you. Keep your blade flying furiously and watch as your Max Combo counter rises in accordance. Should the Goblin horde prove too dangerous, retreat back to your guard troops and lead the horde into a trap.

Realizing that they have been bested, the Goblin cowards retreat into the mountains. You give chase, determined to rid the land of this despicable race, but as you do a landslide seals the path behind you.

Separated from Aspharr's support, you and your guard troops must rendezvous with Aspharr to the north.

Damn! Landslide!

Prepare for combat. Do not retreat. Wipe out every last Goblin! Show them no mercy!

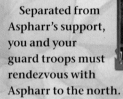

The landslide behind you places you between rocks and a hard place— a hard place full of Goblin vermin. If the previous horde provided enough Orbs to fill your gauge, unleash it now. The attacking Goblin army should provide enough blue Orbs to fill your Orb Spark meter.

If your Orb gauge is not full, take this opportunity to finish filling it up. Then, unleash it and absorb as many blue Orbs as possible.

NOTE

Be very careful in choosing attacks to unleash on your enemies. Activating an Orb Attack (emptying your red Orb gauge) will charge your weapon and infuse you with the power of the Orbs. While charged with an Orb Attack, the enemies you kill release blue Orbs to fill your Orb Spark meter.

Unleashing an Orb Spark (emptying the blue gauge), however, is a way to instantly kill all the enemies directly in front of you. Though an Orb Spark is a more powerful attack, it is not always fool proof.

Do not rush it. Advance slowly.

OBJECTIVE
Join Aspharr at the rally point.

TIP

As always, check the map for a blinking indicator that shows where to go. There are many twists and turns, but the rally point is not far.

The rally point lies to the north. Begin your quest to rejoin Aspharr by regrouping your guard troops and placing them in a defensive posture. The archers take the rear, while the infantry brings up the point.

Carefully tread the fog-laden path ahead into a dark and dank Goblin holy territory. Large pikes with shamanistic totems hang in the fog as if warning incomers. Just as you set foot past their passive warnings, a group of Goblins amasses and rushes at you from all sides.

Rush into the masses and meet them head-on. Set your infantry to defend and your archers to attack. As you wade blood-frenzied into the fray, your archers diminish the Goblin ranks, while your infantry speeds alongside you.

Emerge from the other end of the Goblin army and immediately

about-face to pinch the army between your blade and your archers' rainfall of arrows. Amidst the Goblin army, your infantry gets to work.

March north along the path past the Goblin holy ground and meet with another gaggle of Goblins. Deactivate your guards for a spell and rush into the battle. Claim as many Orbs as possible before leading the Goblins back to your waiting troops.

As the foolish Goblins approach,

they are met with a hail of arrows. While they fall to your archers' expert marksmanship, double back into the Goblin army's center and finish what you started.

Before proceeding, deactivate your troops to keep them stationary. March ahead solo and use your Orb Attack on the next Goblin squad. Should you be fresh out of Orbs, simply treat the Goblins as you would gnats: swat them.

Once finished, attack the Goblin wizards at the head of the next army. If they go unchecked, they pose a great danger to your guards. After killing them off, return to your guards and regroup. In doing so, you draw the rest of the Goblin army into your rested troops.

CAUTION

Another reason for keeping your guards away from Goblin wizards is to keep the wizards from casting a reversal spell on your guards. If they do, the spell causes your troops to turn on you and become enemies.

Press north in relentless pursuit of vengeance, collecting as many Orbs as possible. Stock up and fight the urge to unleash holy hell on your enemies—you'll need a full Orb gauge soon enough.

At the rally point you are welcomed by a large angry Troll. Rest assured, he is there for a fight. Give him and his army one. Immediately unleash your Orb Spark attack and eliminate his bothersome backup. This leaves only you, your support, and the Troll.

Grab whatever power-ups your holy havoc left behind, then turn your attention to the Troll. Wait until your troops lay into him, then accentuate the Troll torture with well-timed sword slashes. Keep you distance; pick at him, then back off when he attacks.

Eventually, Aspharr reaches the rally point, followed by his troops. He provides much-welcomed help in felling the giant Troll.

Use quick strikes and defensive dashes and your attacks will be too much for the Troll. Even after he picks up a large tree trunk, the Troll is trounced by your and Aspharr's efforts.

The Troll has fallen, the Goblin army has been bested. But celebration seems premature as a messenger on the brink of death hobbles onto the battlefield. He falls at Aspharr's feet and pleads for your aid.

The Castle of Varrvazzar has come under siege by Orcs and only you can help. Against your brother's wishes and the messenger's pleas, you decide against a support march to Varrvazzar and instead pursue the Goblin menace toward their stronghold at Fort Wyandeek.

OUTSIDE WYANDEEK

⚔ **Treasure Chest**

Thanks to a messenger who risked his life, Inphyy learns that the Castle of Varrvazzar is under attack. Ignoring the call for aid, Inphyy orders the knights to march for Fort Wyandeek to crush the Goblin base and quell the uprising. Aspharr questions the decision, but Inphyy believes she is making the right choice.

GUARD UNITS
Heavy Infantry (x2)

Don't let them escape!

News of your blood-filled quest must have reached the outlying areas of Wyandeek, because the Goblin army now refuses to fight. A large, scared stream of Goblin fiends tramples across the valley in a weak attempt to escape your justice.

Not content to let the filthy monsters flee, you order your troops to give chase. "Don't let them escape!" you call out, as your followers "Huzzah!" behind you. The chase is on....

OBJECTIVE
Pursue the Goblin troops.

Immediately dash down the countryside behind the fleeing cowards. As they file around the bend ahead, cut the corner and sprint into their ranks. Don't immediately attack the tail of their train; instead slash at the center as you press toward the head of the fleeing Goblin troops.

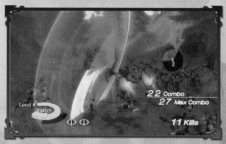

Once at the head, slow down their escape by carving into their numbers. They didn't show your father any mercy—why should you be any different?

You slow their retreat but soon find out that they weren't retreating. No, they were baiting you into a trap. Goblins pour down the hills ahead. Hatchets raised high, teeth gnarling, and with evil in their hearts, they approach.

No matter, this is what you wanted anyway—a large group of Goblins on which to exact revenge. Greet them with your blade as your infantry whittles their numbers.

OBJECTIVE
Destroy the enemy.

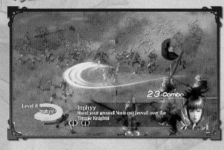

As the sound of metal against metal rings out around you, your rallying cries pierce your troops' ears. "Stand your ground! None can prevail over the Temple Knights!" Your groups rally as you put blade to Goblin flesh. Slice them to ribbons and save up your Orb gauge for a later time, should you fill it up during this skirmish.

Demolish the Goblin vermin with impunity, for they are the ones responsible for the land's unrest—and your father's demise.

Use large sweeping attacks to fell squads in high numbers. As the opposition dwindles, regroup your troops and collect the spoils of war littered about the field. Once properly boosted from bonus items, march forward over the hill.

OBJECTIVE
Find the Goblin camp.

On the hill's other side nestles a large Goblin camp. The Goblin commander in charge of the camp hosts well over 200 troops. Should the camp mobilize, they pose an enormous threat to the neighboring areas. Rather than being intimidated, you see this as great practice for the slaughter you are planning to deliver on Fort Wyandeek.

Crush the forces just outside the gate with your blade, but do not use your Orb gauge yet. The real meat of the battle sits comfortably behind the camp walls. Let them wait; you will bring death on them soon.

OBJECTIVE
Destroy the Goblin troops.

Rush past the camp's walls, and let the Goblin cretins swarm toward you. Bide your time and wait until they are sufficiently pooled in front of you, then use your Orb gauge to power up.

Carve through the enemy horde, collecting blue Orbs as you go. Not only do you deplete the Goblin force at the camp, but you fill up your Orb Spark meter.

Continue the assault on the camp while your guards rush into the fight. Protect your troops, however, by bringing down the nearby archer towers.

The towers are sturdy, but no match for your blade. Be persistent and swing at them bravely, and eventually the towers come tumbling down.

Upon reaching him, unleash your Orb Attack to eliminate his squad. This leaves him all alone for you to face. Scream through him toward his troops and drop them with your Orb-enhanced attacks.

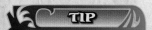

TIP

Bring down the towers quickly; the longer they stand, the longer your troops take damage. Leaping combos like Fly Highland are particularly effective.

OBJECTIVE
Defeat the enemy leader.

After you reduce the Goblin numbers at the camp to virtually nil, the Goblin commander foolishly storms the battlefield with his complement behind him.

Turn your attention to him and carve a path straight to him as you charge across the battleground.

Watch for the commander to cock his hand back as he prepares to deal a blow. As he does, block his attempt or dash away from his range, only to return with a counterattack of your own. Attack with short piercing combos, because large sweeping attacks are wasted on single foes.

Because of your sharp concentrated attacks and well-timed blocks, the commander falls victim to your fierce hatred for all things Goblin.

When his remaining troops see their leader slain, they begin to flee. Intercept them and dispose of the remaining filth.

The Goblin encampment has been eradicated and the road to Fort Wyandeek lies ahead. Though the road ahead is clear, the road behind you is paved in Goblin blood.

FORT WYANDEEK

Treasure Chest

Fending off the Goblin forces along the way, the Temple Knights make their way to Fort Wyandeek. The knights must strike the Goblin stronghold and crush the opposition in order to stamp out the Goblin uprising. But for Inphyy, this day will also mean avenging her father's murder.

GUARD UNITS
Infantry
Archers

Charge ahead and search out the first of the two Goblin captains to the west. Small groups of enemy archers are littered between you and your first target. Slash them down on your way to the captain.

As you charge ahead, your guard troops—and those of the other generals, Aspharr and Heppe—follow in the near distance. Press toward your target, obliterating small squads in your way.

You reach the first Goblin captain with hatred in your heart and vengeance on the tip of your blade. Since your troops are still behind you, use a lunge attack to deliver the first blow on the Goblin captain.

As you lunge at him, you expose yourself to his troops. Fret not—yours should be close behind now. Swat his troops away and focus your attacks on the captain.

Finish off the captain before more of his grunts pour in from the cliffside. After destroying the captain with a few devastating combos, back away from the battle and let the troops collide with the incoming Goblin support.

By distancing yourself for a second, you prevent getting surrounded in close quarters by enemies. As you turn back into the battle, rush in and swipe at the Goblin grunts. If you have a full Orb gauge, unleash an Orb Attack now. The resulting blue Orbs should provide a good start in filling your Orb Spark meter for later.

Rush back into the valley to meet with the next wave of blade fodder. As you traverse the valley, draw the oncoming horde to the right of the large stone. Doing so brings them into a very narrow area that bunches them up.

Here, use strong sweeps to drop as many of the clustered enemies as possible. Let your troops handle your fallout Goblins. If you drew them into the narrow path correctly, a few short swings of your blade should eliminate all but a few of the Goblin devils.

Deactivate your troops and venture ahead on your own. The way to the second Goblin captain leads through a large hill with plenty of dangerous boulders waiting. Leave your support behind and charge the small squad at the base of the hill ahead.

The Goblin fools behind the squad release the first two boulders and trample their own men. Meanwhile, your troops patiently wait for your orders from the safety of the valley behind you.

Continue up the hill toward the next Goblin captain. Aspharr and his men follow you, while yours stay at the hill's base.

Draw out the remaining armies and entice the captain to release the next few boulders onto an empty hillside. Reach the captain atop the hill and destroy him with a few combos. Aspharr helps out, but the captain is yours to deal with.

With both captains dead, the main gate opens up, granting entrance into the next area of Fort Wyandeek. Rush back down the hill, regroup your troops, and cut past the few enemy archer troops that show up.

Saunter through the main gate and penetrate deeper into the Goblin stronghold. They can't hide forever!

OBJECTIVE
Find and defeat the Orc corporal.

Beyond the gate is another open area bordered by a large hill to the right. As you cross the gate a swarm of Goblins comes streaming down the hillside ready for action. Hold your ground, set your troops to defend, and meet the Goblins head on.

Wait until they finish crashing down around you and then unleash an Orb Attack as soon as possible. Maximize your Orb Attack so as to not waste it on a few enemies that grant piddly few blue Orbs. If you use it early enough, the remaining troops grant enough blue Orbs to fill your Orb Spark meter. Save it.

With your Orb Spark meter full, hurry across the valley to meet with the Orc corporal. Dash into his ranks with your sword at your side. Don't strike just yet. Dash around his ranks quick enough to avoid taking damage but long enough to draw out the rest of his troops from the surrounding hills.

When they come rushing out, dash outside of the corporal's range and turn back into the mess of menaces. Quickly unleash your Orb Spark to instantly eliminate the Orc corporal and his goons. The next central gate opens.

OBJECTIVE
Destroy the archers.

The next gate leads to an ambush! Companies of archers wait with their bows drawn and their strings tight. If your troops rush into their aim, they will be picked off without ever landing a single blow.

Rush into the ranged combatants and break them up. Eliminate the threat and allow your troops to engage the other squads without worrying about being impaled by a rogue arrow.

Lead your army west toward the fort's westernmost edge. There you find a lone sorceress engaged in combat with a group of Goblin bullies.

Protected by the Light, Tyurru the sorceress uses Water magic to wash the Goblins clean of their evil constitution. Lend her a helping hand and finish off the remaining Goblin threat.

Lead your army back to the east side of the fort. A large canyon with a single rope bridge grants access to Wyandeek's heart.

Unfortunately, Pwucks destroy the bridge as you do battle with the small group of enemy archers. The group of archers is not a huge threat; eliminate them while your troops catch up.

Destroying the enemy archers grants you access past the next large central gate. Run through the gate and meet with another Orc corporal to the right of the gate.

As you approach, you spy a tall dark figure, also protected by the Light, engaging the Orc corporal. The figure is Klarrann, priest of Varrgandd. Aid the holy man as he wages war on the Orc corporal. Meanwhile, leave the surrounding troops to your guards. Once you drop the Orc corporal, engage the other enemies on the battlefield on your way to the next central gate.

Finally having reached the Goblin stronghold, you find that the area is rife with Goblins. Grunts, archers, even civilian Goblins all seek refuge here. No matter—a Goblin is a Goblin.

Aspharr takes notice of the civilian presence and hesitates, but he forgets that he who hesitates dies. Besides, all Goblins are the same.

BRANCHING TALE

Before proceeding straight ahead toward the Goblin altar, turn left and attack the huts on the western edge of the fort. Aside from pillaging the village and helping yourself to the contents of the treasure chests, you rid yourself of Goblins that may pose a threat in the future.

Unfortunately, Aspharr doesn't see it your way. His feelings for the women and children Goblins cloud his judgment. He feels you have gone too far this time. Has he forgotten that these are the people who killed your father?

Before attacking the Goblin altar, deactivate your troops. As before, approach the hill alone to draw the large boulders and keep them from harming your troops. Once all the boulders have been launched, run back to your troops and reactivate them.

Lead them past the Goblin reinforcements up to the altar where the priests await. Your squad can be slower than you, so slice past the few groups on the hill leading up to the altar and leave the rest to your squad to clean up.

Atop the hill, use an Orb Attack to eliminate the wizards' guards. With their support troops out of the way, focus on the three wizards. Watch for their attack spells and interrupt them before they can finish their maledictions.

Fort Wyandeek falls at your feet and the Goblin uprising is all but quelled. Suddenly, a mysterious fog comes over the fort. You call on the power of Yesperratt to send the Goblin filth where they belong—to their graves.

While Aspharr once again complains about your actions, a messenger brings word that the Goblin king, Dwykfarrio, fled from Varrgandd to the flatlands. You know where you must go next.

PHOLYA FLATLANDS

Treasure Chest

Fort Wyandeek is destroyed; it is a place of carnage and death. But Goblin king Dwykfarrio has amassed immense forces in the Pholya Flatlands, made up of soldiers from the Outlands. The battle between the Army of Light and the Army of Darkness is about to begin, with both sides seeking their form of justice.

GUARD UNITS Heavy Infantry (x2)

The sky over Pholya looks surprisingly serene. A light breeze bends the vibrant green blades of grass, and the sun peers out from behind harmless clouds. Had this been any other day, families would be littered about on picnic lunches.

Since the battle can get very hectic, work up and down the riverbank to make sure you are helping every general's guards. Let your heavy infantry stay rested.

It's not long before a Troll joins the fight and comes careening down into the river from the opposite bank. Run back to your troops and regroup; they're going to come in handy.

Today, forces have gathered on the Pholya Flatlands and they must be stopped. Should any of these scoundrels survive, they are sure to inspire more uprisings in the future. It's time the Temple Knights brought peace back to the Pholya Flatlands.

OBJECTIVE
Destroy the enemy.

Immediately deactivate your heavy infantry and march ahead toward the river. Join the other generals' support guards and leap into the fray. Slash at the enemy grunts and rack up as many Orbs as you can to fill up your gauge.

Lead your troops across the river toward the enemy Trolls. Your infantry collides with the Troll's squad. Engage the Troll in combat before his powerful advances lay waste to your troops.

Use leaping combo attacks to strike at the Troll consistently. Moves like Vermillion Full Moon or Fly Highland are extremely effective. After defeating one Troll, regroup your troops and attack the next.

OBJECTIVE
Destroy the Arphann that control the dragons.

Seeing that the Trolls are defeated, Dwykfarrio sends dragons into the fight. Their fire sweeps are extremely dangerous, as they not only cause damage but also interrupt your attacks.

They do have a weakness, however; the Arphann that control them are just as susceptible to your blade as any other Goblin. Immediately execute an Orb Attack to kill the Arphann and rid yourself of the dragon threat. One Orb Attack will not eliminate the entire Arphann troop, but there are more than enough to refill the Orb Attack gauge for another attack.

A second army of the Temple Knights joins the effort but, alas, does not last long. Just as soon as the knights set foot on the field, they are destroyed. Don't let them die in vain.

OBJECTIVES
Repel Dwykfarrio.
Defeat Dwingvatt.

As Dwykfarrio's forces dwindle, he calls on his second in command, Dwingvatt. Dwingvatt leads his own group of Goblins down the hill to attack from behind.

Dwingvatt is so confident in his abilities that he rushes ahead of his troops by more than 100 paces. Luckily, you have support and aren't arrogant enough to leave it behind.

Clash blades with Dwingvatt as he comes running down the hill. Beware of his dash attack and sidestep it as he lunges at you. Once he is past, attack him from behind with a strong combo.

Sooner rather than later, his troops arrive. Keep an eye on Dwingvatt, as it is easy to lose him in the fray. Knock the enemy troops aside as you search out Dwingvatt to land another combo chain.

As you continue to fight Dwingvatt and his goons, place a high priority on Goblin wizards. Eliminate them first, after attacking Dwingvatt, then refocus your efforts on the Goblin leader.

Use an Orb Attack or an Orb Spark to eliminate the rest of the Goblin troops from the field. The sooner you do, the more guards you have at your disposal to help in the fight against Dwingvatt and Dwykfarrio later.

Once Dwingvatt stands alone, let your remaining squad surround him. Work around the fight, picking at him and backing off before he can land his own combos. As your troops distract him, you subtract him.

Another victim to your bloodlust, Dwingvatt falls limp to the ground. You outmatched him and his guards. Now only Dwykfarrio remains. He approaches from the northeast, so if you are low on health, search the surrounding area for chests with HP power-ups. If not, run up to Dwykfarrio and say hello...with your blade.

Just like you, Dwykfarrio doesn't waste time in drawing his blades. Lunge at him to attack, but dash away from him before he unleashes his spike attack. The Goblin king has many dangerous attacks. With one he pounds the ground and raises power spikes from the area around his feet, and in another he unleashes a wave of energy from his fist.

Continue dashing away from his attacks and returning with combos of your own. Juggle him as much as possible with your blade to quickly deplete his health bar.

Being the wily Goblin that he is, he realizes he is outmatched and swiftly speeds away after dodging a deadly blow. If he gets away again, he will never be caught. He must be stopped once and for all!

YWA-UE-UAR FOREST

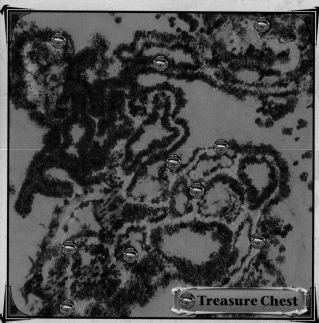

Treasure Chest

In the midst of the fierce battle at the Pholya Flatlands, Inphyy finds the Goblin king Dwykfarrio running for his life. He heads into Ywa-Ue-Uar Forest. Inphyy takes a handful of Temple Knights and pursues him. The land they now tread is also known as the Forbidden Forest.

GUARD UNITS
Heavy Infantry
Pikemen

Before setting off into the Forbidden Forest, you give your doubting brother the responsibility of bringing up the rear while you and Heppe take point. Though Heppe is surprised at your command, Aspharr seems less than pleased.

The fact is, guarding the rear is crucial to survival—the only way to avoid being sandwiched by clever enemies.

Deactivate your squad and march ahead. A small group of enemies approaches from ahead and another one flanks you from the right. The group in front is much closer, so attack it first.

With the path ahead clear, return to your troops and lead them down the path on the right, due east. Meet with the second enemy group and dispatch your foes.

Regroup your guards and stampede up the path to the northeast. Other small packs of enemies approach from the adjacent paths; stop briefly

to deal with them and continue on your search for Dwykfarrio.

Charge north up the hill and take on another small squad of Goblin marauders. Don't worry about your troops being far behind; the enemy groups

ahead are small and manageable.

Let your troops finally catch up as you reach the three-way fork in the road. There you will be met by multiple enemy groups attempting to pinch you in.

Allow them to group at the fork's junction, then clean the area with large broad strokes of your blade. Orcs approach from one end, enemy

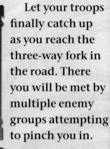

archers from another, so split your troops between the different avenues and take the third on your own.

After surviving the three-pronged attack, collect your guards and charge up the middle path. Crash through a few enemy archers with ease and press on in your Goblin hunt.

You spy Dwykfarrio up ahead but are not able to apprehend or engage him. Instead, he disappears deeper into the forest, leaving you to contend with more of his troops.

Set your guards on attack mode and leap into the center of the battle. Crush as many enemies as you can until you fill your Orb Attack gauge. Save it for now; you will need it soon enough.

Suddenly, a large beastly creature waddles into the battle. It's Ppakk the Third, king of the Pwucks. He has brought half of his kingdom, it seems, to aid the Goblin king.

Back away from the conflict and let his Pwucks crash into your guards. Once the pack of Pwucks has engaged in battle, let them cluster in tight before you unleash your Orb Attack on the entire Pwuck kingdom.

Let the Orb gauge empty as you nearly instantly kill the entire opposition. The resulting blue Orbs should be more than enough to fill the rest of your Orb Spark meter. Once it is full, save it.

With his entire army gone, Ppakk the Third is defenseless and at the mercy of you and your guards. Let your troops bait him and sneak up on him from behind.

Use Fly Highland repeatedly to speedily deplete his health bar. The high-flying combo not only lands numerous strikes on his head but also knocks him to the floor, rendering him incapable of dealing a single blow. As he is about to get up, deliver another Fly Highland combo. Continue this until he stays down.

Ppakk has fallen, but Dwykfarrio has yet to stop running. As Ppakk dies, you're whisked away to a far northwest corner of the Forbidden Forest and are about to find out why it is "forbidden."

The Army of Darkness has amassed forces in this region of the forest and now stands in direct opposition to you. Engage the dark army and dodge its gassy sphere attack. Use attacks like Seraph Butterfly that keep you from their level of attack and cause major damage to multiple enemies. After putting up a solid offensive, the Army of Darkness retreats.

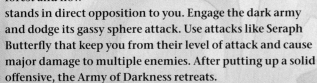

Things clear up, briefly, and Aspharr returns. A strange stupor graces his face as he approaches, and he seems reluctant to respond with any enthusiasm.

He again begins to express his revulsion at your recent behavior. Caught up in the frenzy of his own maniacal ranting, he lunges at you

with his spear only to disappear into the forest without causing any damage or actually landing a blow! Was it a threat or a threatened brother's childish posturing? No—he simply doesn't understand you.

Goblin king shall be yours!

If you have an Orb Attack or an Orb Spark, now is the time to use it.

Not all is lost, though. Heppe returns with good news. Dwykfarrio was seen running to the northeast, and Heppe sent scouts to surround him. Finally, the

Set forth to the northeast edge of the Forbidden Forest! Stop to gather Heppe's troops along the way, but be careful; the Goblin wizards can temporarily turn them against you.

If your troops got hit by the Goblin spell, wait until it wears off, then chop down the Goblin threat.

Eliminate the Goblin wizards first. Then splash across the marsh toward the enemy archers. As you approach, they break ranks and come after you.

Greet them with your blade and rob them of their Orbs. Behind the archers are more wizards. Target them right away to keep them from zapping you with their evil spells.

Regroup with your troops and charge farther northeast. The path ahead sweeps around into a dead end at the northeastern-most edge of the forest. As you reach the U-bend in the path, you come upon a clearing.

Just beyond the clearing, at the end of the U-bend, waits one more small group of Goblins. Kill them before they do any damage to your troops.

Just beyond the clearing, at the forest's end, stands Dwykfarrio. He has nowhere to run this time. He *must* face you.

OBJECTIVE
Defeat Dwykfarrio.

In a last-ditch attempt to defend, he sets his last group of Goblins on you. Let them collide with your group of guards, but don't let your guards take all of the damage. Assist them in their valiant efforts while Dwykfarrio approaches.

When the area is clean of enemy interlopers, turn your full attention to Dwykfarrio and reintroduce him to your blade. Just as before, use leaping combos to chop his health and dashes to escape his retaliations. Block when possible, but mainly slice at him and back away, allowing your support to distract him while you refocus your attacks.

Eventually Dwykfarrio falls, a defeated Goblin king. Even he is no match for your blade and must now pay the price for your father's murder. An eye for an eye, a Goblin king for your father.

Aspharr arrives just in time to witness you drive your blade into Dwykfarrio's weakened body. As expected, Aspharr feebly attempts to keep you from completing your duty. But alas, it is what must be done—for your father, for your people, and for peace.

Your mission is complete, your father is avenged, and the Goblin race is no more. Destiny has been fulfilled, yet there is an emptiness inside—as if all the hatred that has been driving you has suddenly taken physical form and left your body, leaving a void.

Slowly a dark mist forms around you. It angrily swirls about you, engulfing you in its violent chaos. What is this mist? Can it be your anger taking physical form? Is it your darkness taking over? Aspharr looks on helplessly....

Age:
19

Class:
Knight

Weapon:
Lance

Orb Spark:
Light

Aspharr is a compassionate man who does not favor conflict. Although he fights well, he continues to wonder what the true nature of justice is. He worries mostly for his younger sister, Inphyy. His weapon is a lance.

He loves his sister, Inphyy, but has mixed feelings; he knows they aren't related by blood. He also has misgivings about the cause of "justice for humans only" that is driving the war.

VITAL STATISTICS

Category	Level 1	Level 2	Level 3	Level 4	Level 5	Level 6	Level 7	Level 8	Level 9
Default Attack Point	100	110	121	133	146	161	177	195	214
Default HP	1,200	1,530	2,320	3,332	4,600	5,500	8,800	14,266	22,004
Default Defense Point	20	22	24	27	29	32	35	39	43
Default Rate of Critical Hit	10	11	12	13	14	15	16	17	18

COMBO ATTACKS

Aspharr's attacks befit his demeanor: careful, graceful, but powerful at the same time. His lance reaches far but can also impale enemies at close range. Much like Aspharr himself, his weapon seeks justice.

Level 1

Aspharr's level 1 combos are powerful attack chains meant to fell multiple enemies. However, moves like Upper Swing are also great for launching single enemies high into the air to begin juggling combos. Practice the timing on Aspharr's level 1 combos and 1,000-hit combos will be the norm.

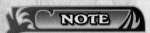

> When doing a combo attack, execute button presses separated by commas in quick succession.
>
> If the move says ", then" or ", press", allow the final move to finish before pressing the next button command.

Move	Execution
Charge	Ⓡ
Destroyer Chain	ⓨ,ⓨ,ⓨ,ⓨ
Divine Knight	During Orb Attack, press ⓧ
Gala Impact	In mid-jump, press ⓨ
Lancer Storm	ⓧ,ⓧ,ⓧ,ⓨ (press the last ⓨ repeatedly)
Shining Flare	During Orb Attack, press ⓨ
Slide Slash	ⓨ,ⓨ,ⓧ
Sonic Impact	Ⓡ, then press ⓧ
Swing Rush	ⓧ,ⓧ,ⓧ,ⓧ
Tornado Slash	ⓨ,ⓨ,ⓨ,ⓧ,ⓧ
Upper Swing	ⓧ,ⓧ,ⓨ,ⓨ,

Level 2

Level 2 combos are shorter, quicker attacks with high-impact potential. Flash Lance is a particularly powerful strike that sends out numerous bolts of light from the tip of Aspharr's lance; use it against boss enemies to great success.

Move	Execution
Dead-end Break	When stabbing an enemy with ⓨ,ⓧ, press ⓧ
Dead-end Strike	ⓨ,ⓧ
Flash Lance	ⓧ,ⓨ (press the last ⓨ repeatedly)
Spiral Dive	In mid-jump, press ⓧ

Level 3

Though only two moves are added at level 3, they enhance both your aerial and ground attacks.

Move	Execution
Dead-end Turn	ⓨ,ⓧ, then press Ⓐ
Tornado Impact	ⓨ,ⓨ,ⓨ,ⓧ,ⓧ,ⓧ

Level 4

At level 4, Aspharr begins to realize his true potential as a knight. He gains numerous new moves, all of which are excellent ways to dispatch large groups of enemies.

Move	Execution
Double-slide Slash	ⓨ,ⓨ,ⓧ,ⓧ
Divine Burst	ⓧ,ⓧ,ⓧ + ⓨ repeatedly, then press ⓧ (drains Orb Attack gauge)
Shining Spear	ⓨ,ⓨ,ⓨ,ⓧ,ⓧ,ⓨ (drains Orb Attack gauge)
Sonic Strike	Ⓡ, then press ⓨ
Spiral Charge	In mid-jump, press ⓧ,ⓧ
Upper Slash	ⓧ,ⓧ,ⓨ,ⓨ,ⓨ

> Though Divine Burst is one of the most difficult combos to execute in the game, it is also one of the most dazzling to behold.

Level 5

Having reached a high point at level 4, Aspharr's abilities are enhanced with two new maneuvers at level 5.

Move	Execution
Dead-end Cyclone	When stabbing an enemy (ⓨ,ⓧ), press ⓨ
Upper Flash Lance	ⓧ,ⓧ,ⓨ,ⓨ,ⓧ

Level 6

Level 6 introduces three enhancements to Aspharr's Dead-end series of attacks. His Upper Twist Slash is an extremely useful combo that causes a great deal of damage and keeps you off the battlefield ground.

Move	Execution
Dead-end Burst	ⓨ,ⓧ, then ⓧ+Ⓐ (drains Orb Attack gauge)
Dead-end Charge	ⓨ,ⓧ, then Ⓡ
Dead-end Swing	ⓨ,ⓧ, then during Ⓡ,ⓧ
Upper Twist Slash	ⓧ,ⓧ,ⓨ,ⓨ,ⓨ,ⓨ

Level 7

Aspharr's level 7 additions are an impact maneuver, a charge, and a slash. All are enhanced versions of previous moves.

Move	Execution
Dead-end Impact	Ⓨ,Ⓧ, then Ⓡⓣ,Ⓐ
Double-spiral Charge	In mid-jump, press Ⓧ,Ⓧ,Ⓨ
Triple Slide Slash	Ⓨ,Ⓨ,Ⓧ,Ⓧ,Ⓧ

Level 8

Though only one combo joins the repertoire at this level, the Holy Spear is extremely powerful.

Move	Execution
Holy Spear	Ⓨ,Ⓨ,Ⓨ,Ⓧ,Ⓧ,Ⓨ

Level 9

Aspharr's final move is a blast of Orb energy that devastates the battlefield. Use it carefully, though, as it depletes your Orb Attack gauge.

Move	Execution
Shining Blast	Ⓧ,Ⓧ,Ⓧ,Ⓨ,Ⓧ (drains Orb Attack gauge)

WEAPONS

Aspharr's lances are strong, far-reaching weapons with powerful heads that can pound, impale, or even slash through enemies.

Temple Spear

Level 1

This spear is carried only by Temple Knights; it is Aspharr's default weapon.

Earth Pike

Level 2

A deadly lance that shatters both enemies and earth, the Earth Pike boosts both Attack range and critical rate by 10 percent.

Knight Lance

Level 2

A classic Temple Knight weapon, the Knight Lance increases Attack power by 20 percent, Defense power by 20 percent, and Speed by 10 percent.

Water Spike

Level 3

This beautiful blue-rippled blade looks like waves in the water. When Water Spike is equipped, Attack power goes up 20 percent, Attack range goes up 30 percent, and Orb appear rate increases by 15 percent.

Blue Lance

Level 3

A lightning lance that emits blue flashes, Blue Lance enhances Attack power by 10 percent, Attack range by 40 percent, critical rate by 30 percent, and Speed by 15 percent.

Bryunak

Level 5

A supernatural weapon known as the Lance of Light, Bryunak increases Attack power by 70 percent, Speed by 30 percent, Attack range by 50 percent, and red Orb appearance by 30 percent with Orb Spark.

Crystal Spear

Level 5

This divine lance bears the power of crystal. It boosts Attack power by 30 percent, Attack range by 50 percent, and Orb Attack duration by 20 percent.

Neredis Spear

Level 7

An ancient spear that can split the sea, the Neredis Spear augments Attack range by 40 percent, critical rate by 50 percent, and Orb gauge charge rate by 30 percent.

Weapon Locations and Conditions

Weapon	Location/Condition
Temple Spear	Default weapon
Earth Pike	Treasure chest in Eaurvarria Mission
Knight Lance	Dropped in Eaurvarria Mission
Water Spike	Treasure chest at the beginning of Varrvazarr Mission
Blue Lancer	Treasure chest at the beginning of Wyandeek Mission
Crystal Spear	Treasure chest in Wyandeek Mission
Nereids Spear	Treasure chest in Ywa-Ue-Uar Mission
Bryunak	Clear Varrvazarr Mission with S Rank

THE QUEST FOR JUSTICE

Aspharr's quest is one of justice. Stories passed on tell of an Orb that was once split in two. Goblin tales blame humans for the Orb's divide, while human legend places the blame on Goblin shoulders. After the split, the Orb's evil half possessed the Goblin king, Dwykfarrio. It is Aspharr's duty to rejoin the Orb halves and bring balance back to the land.

DIVINE VARRFARRINN

🛡 **Treasure Chest**

Aspharr is not eager to face Inphyy, his younger sister, in a match to decide the next leader of the Temple Knights. But sensing that Inphyy is too emotionally invested in its outcome, he knows he has no choice but to fight to protect his sister's feelings.

As you stand at the top of the hill, your loyal troops wait below. You remind them that although this is a practice battle, the outcome is of greatest importance.

You encourage them to fight with all their heart and let their hearts guide them to pull back when things might go too far. You seek to capture the enemy, not destroy it. Your blades should not taste blood.

OBJECTIVE
Defeat the enemies atop the hill.

Rush into the battle just behind your troops. Your first encounter is with Heppe. Disable him quickly with a few well-delivered blows of your lance.

He falls swiftly to your charge, but his troops remain. Aid your guards in diminishing their numbers on your way to stop the enemies atop the hill.

The archers on the hilltop are your targets. Flank them as you approach and dive headlong into their center. Swing your lance about and eliminate the first archer squad.

Once done, flank the other squad of archers on the opposite hill. They too fall quickly to your lance, and are no longer a threat to your troops below.

OBJECTIVE
Reinforce the troops in battle.

Rush back down from the hills to support the troops in the trenches below. Watch for the squad with the most enemy opposition and charge in!

After you eliminate the opposition below, Inphyy rushes into the skirmish. Her guards follow not far behind. It's time to decide who will lead these Temple Knights. You must face her head on.

OBJECTIVE
Defeat the enemy general.

As Inphyy boldly charges at you, turn your attention to her and rush at her at full speed. Prepare for a full-speed collision with your sister. This is for the leadership of the Temple Knights!

If you have filled your Orb Attack gauge, use it on her and her troops just as she nears. Pummel her with

as many Orb-charged attacks as possible, but make sure you immobilize her troops completely. Once Inphyy is the only opposition standing, finish off the rest of her health bar with strong combo attacks like Destroyer Chain.

Inphyy falls to your lance, just as the troops did before. She lies defeated on the battlefield as you stand victorious over her.

She concedes that your skills are great, but in her childlike way, she jokes that you have much farther to go. You are the new leader of the Temple Knights; hopefully she can learn to accept that.

Instead of advancing straight to Fort Wyandeek, the Goblin army stands strong at the Eaurvarria Mountains. You would rather avoid another confrontation. Truth be told, you would rather avoid the war altogether, but you don't have much choice.

You prepare your troops for battle at the base of the mountain range; the Goblins stand between you and peace. This is an unfortunate but necessary step.

EAURVARRIA MOUNTAINS

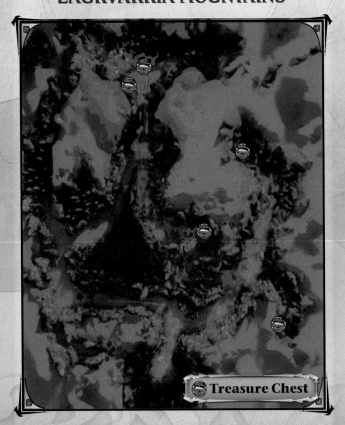

🔹 **Treasure Chest**

In a duel to become leader of the Temple Knights, Aspharr now notices that Inphyy's confidence has grown. Can he keep his sister under control? A bit uneasy, Aspharr leads the Temple Knights to the Eaurvarria Mountains, where the Goblin army is currently advancing.

Tear into the Goblin troops with your lance. They are numerous and easy to plow through. Simply use your power attacks to brush the grunts aside and absorb their Orbs.

Continue racking up combos on your combo counter while simultaneously eliminating Goblins and filling your Orb gauge for later use.

**GUARD UNITS
Infantry
Archers**

The Goblin army stalls as long as possible before taking flight into the mountains. Inphyy, in all her impulsive glory, immediately gives chase.

The Goblin Army is full of cowards after all! Commander Aspharr, I'll pursue them!

333 Kills

As the frightened Goblins and your tempestuous sister disappear into the mountains, a landslide blocks you from following. You need to regroup with Inphyy at the rally point, but you must take a detour.

Hold it, Inphyy!

333 Kills

Continue moving east along the mountain path until you arrive on sacred Goblin ground. Under normal circumstances you would find a path around this area, but you must move hastily to catch up with Inphyy.

OBJECTIVE
Join Inphyy at the rally point.

108 Combo
711 Max Combo
180 Kills

The rally point lies to the north. About-face to take the eastern route, as it wends its way north.

As expected, another Goblin group attacks from the east. Let your guards clash steel with the Goblin group as you dash past the first wave and meet with the second Goblin group. Absorb the remaining Orbs and unleash an Orb Attack on the rest of the troops.

84 Combo
711 Max Combo
272 Kills

OBJECTIVE
Find and destroy the Goblin wizard.

711 Max Combo
333 Kills

711 Max Combo
333 Kills

Regroup with your troops and advance into the Goblin territory. As you set foot on the sacred ground, Goblins attack once again. Two small squads attack from the north, while another two flank you from the west.

Split your troops to defend against the northern attackers while you collide with the enemies from the west. After eliminating your attackers, regroup and defend your area against another wave of assailants.

Before proceeding north, release your troops and let them rest. Turn west and follow the path as it heads north, toward the rally point.

As you advance, beware of the boulders up ahead. Draw out the Goblin presence and free the boulders to bowl them flat. Clean up whatever Goblin presence remains when the boulders pass and eliminate the Goblin wizard.

CAUTION

Be careful when releasing the boulders. If you stand too close to the boulders when you release them, you risk taking damage.

Return to the base of the sacred ground and recall your guards. You will need them at the rally point just around the bend.

Backtrack up the northwest path toward the rally point. This time, however, release the boulders on the other side of the hill and eliminate the attacking

Goblin horde. As before, finish off the remaining Goblins, should any survive.

Three more small enemy groups stand between you and the rendezvous point. Valiantly fight your way past them and ensure that as many of your guards survive as possible.

OBJECTIVE
Destroy the enemy.

March north until you reach the rally point. Inphyy arrives at the rendezvous point at a frenzied pace, which unfortunately leads her straight into a group of Goblins.

Before she takes too much damage, unleash an Orb attack and eliminate the Goblin squads. Inphyy may be rash, but she is still your younger sister and your responsibility.

Just as you finish saving Inphyy's hide, she speeds off again in search of more Goblin blood. What is this bloodlust that makes her so selfish on the battlefield?

Chase Inphyy and lead your troops into battle. It may seem unfair that you risk your soldiers' lives to protect your younger, impulsive sister, but these are the decisions you must make as leader of the Temple Knights.

Charge into battle and collect a few more blue Orbs. After filling your Orb Spark meter, let an Orb Spark loose on the enemy and clear the area.

With the area clear, you send Inphyy east to escort a messenger back. From the west another Goblin squad storms down the hillside. Their leader is a Troll.

Defeat the Troll within 90 seconds so that the messenger and Inphyy may arrive safely. Use leaping combos on the large beast to fell him quickly. Do not allow him to grab hold of a large tree trunk nearby, lest he lay your troops to waste with it. Concentrate on the Troll while your men take care of the other Goblins.

You are amazing, Brother. Your strength is worthy of your title as commanding officer.

Inphyy arrives with the messenger safely in tow. He collapses to the ground and brings news of a siege upon the Castle of Varrvazzarr. Though your path leads north to Fort Wyandeek, he begs for you to march south to the Castle of Varrvazzar and provide help. As leader of the Temple Knights, it is your decision to make.

The Temple Knights... of The Divine Varrfarrinn...?

BRANCHING TALE

As Inphyy suggests, give your following decision due thought. If you abandon your mission at Fort Wyandeek, the Goblin uprising will strengthen, and Dwykfarrio's dark Orb power will grow.

However, if you ignore the messenger's pleas for help, Varrvazzar will fall and thousands will die. The choice is not always so clear for a man of power, but it is the ability to calmly make these life-changing decisions without letting emotions cloud your judgment that makes you leader of the Temple Knights.

CASTLE OF VARRVAZZAR

Treasure Chest

The first line of defense against the Outlands, the Castle of Varrvazzar would let a flood of enemy forces through if it were to fall. Half knowing the situation is already dire, Aspharr travels to Varrvazzar's aid as the proud leader of the mighty Temple Knights.

GUARD UNITS
Infantry
Pikemen

The Castle of Varrvazzar is an ice palace. The surrounding area is laden with snow, and its Ice Gates are the castle's first line of defense.

Upon your arrival you find that the Ice Gates have been breached and the castle is under siege. You introduce yourself to Lord Vyden, steward of Varrvazzar, and offer your help. He graciously accepts.

I am Aspharr of the Temple Knights. We have heard of the attack and have come help!

OBJECTIVES
Aid Vyertenn.
Destroy the Gewgs.

A gaggle of Gewgs attacks Vyertenn, a mysterious but clearly important man, and his men. As promised, rush in and aid them. The Gewgs are strong, but their numbers have been reduced by Vyertenn and his men. Help him finish off the Gewg forces by mashing the remaining Gewgs with your lance.

A few short combos should do the trick. Otherwise, rush in and spear a Gewg, then swing it around to squash the rest. Just outside the skirmish with the Gewgs, enemy archer Gewgs begin to pick apart your troops. Rush out and disband the archers by assaulting their ranks.

OBJECTIVES
Aid Vyarrhertenn!
Defeat Ppakk the Third.

As the last of the encroaching Gewgs fall to your might, Vyertenn introduces himself. He is the son of Vyden, and is a very proud man. He might not have asked for your help, but he isn't going to turn you away.

Ppakk the Third, king of the Pwucks, has arrived and joined the battle. His size is as impressive as his army, for they may look like swamp-dwelling frogs, but they are extremely skilled warriors.

Isolate the king by nullifying his troops first. Use an Orb Attack, or an Orb Spark if you have one, to leave the king standing alone. Once he is, use high-flying combos to knock him down. After he falls, immediately strike with ground attacks before he can get up. If your timing is right, you can force him to withdraw before he ever lands a blow on you.

After Ppakk withdraws, rejoin Vyarrhertenn and fend off another wave of Goblin fiends. They aren't the only ones that want a fight. Dragons join the effort, and below them are those controlling them: the Arphann.

OBJECTIVES
Aid Vyarrhertenn!
Destroy the Arphann.

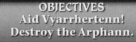

Turn right and sprint over to the right of the castle and meet with the Arphann. Leave your pikemen behind to provide support should any more hostiles arrive. Lead your infantry to the Arphann and punish them.

OBJECTIVES
Join Lord Vydenn!
Defeat the Orc chieftain, Leuu!

The dragons may have fled when their masters fell, but the fight is long from over. Orcs join the other Outland groups to help bring down the Castle of Varrvazzar. Led by their chieftain, Leuu, the Orcs are large, beastly creatures with great strength and an angry disposition.

Chieftain Leuu is an extremely powerful leader. The best way to defeat him is to single him out. If you have an Orb Attack or an Orb Spark, use it against his men and leave the chieftain to fend for himself.

If you didn't manage to get all of his Orc troops, leave the rest to your guards, then push Leuu outside of the battle lines and slap him around with your lance.

His attacks are extremely destructive, so the best strategy to defeat him is to keep him off his feet. Use long juggling combos to knock him in the air and keep him from delivering his own blows.

Just like Ppakk before him, this leader takes flight as soon as his life is in danger. Let him flee; you will get another chance at finishing this fight.

The Gewg were defeated, Ppakk fled, the Arphann fell, and even the Orc chieftain withdrew, but Varrvazzar paid a heavy price. Lord Vydenn lies wounded on the ground, his side bleeding.

He is about to give up hope, but you offer to continue helping. The castle is about to fall, but the Ice Gates still need to be sealed. You will make sure your Temple Knights seal the gates before more Outlanders arrive.

Just as expected, more Goblins arrive. This time they are led by Dwingvatt, Dwykfarrio's right-hand man.

OBJECTIVE
Defeat Dwingvatt.

Finding Dwingvatt in the mess of Goblin invaders can be difficult. Rush into the battle and clear out as many Goblins as you can before Dwingvatt finds you.

Once he does, welcome him to the battle like you did Ppakk and Leuu. Knock him into the air and bring him down with your powerful combos.

TIP

Watch Lord Vydenn's health bar carefully; if he falls, your mission is over. Stay near him to ensure he isn't taking too much damage.

Dwingvatt's no different from the generals you defeated before him. He, too, flees before you can finish him off. He vows revenge as he scampers away, but he is the least of your worries right now.

A soldier arrives with news of Dwykfarrio's arrival at the Pholya Flatlands. You must make your way there to cut him off before he advances.

BRANCHING TALE
Should you choose to attack Fort Wyandeek, read on.

FORT WYANDEEK

Treasure Chest

Though ill at ease about the fate of the Castle of Varrvazzar, Aspharr decides not to ride to its aid. Instead, he will strike the Goblin army base, with hopes of ending war and to obey his orders from Ectvarr. He also wants to show Inphyy his strong resolve as the leader of the Temple Knights.

GUARD UNITS
Infantry (x2)

OBJECTIVE
Defeat the two Goblin captains.

You march on Fort Wyandeek's doorstep and find a large Goblin resistance force waiting. They aren't going to grant you access to the fort that easily. Two Goblin captains guard the outer gate. Defeat them to get inside.

Your first step is to eliminate the Goblin captain at the eastern edge of the fort. He is the closest to you and so should be your first target. Dash across the central area of the fort and take out his first line of defense.

He falls easily to strong attacks like Triple Slide Slash. Let your guards stand their ground while you finish off the captain.

Do an about-face and return to the valley. There you encounter even more Goblin troops. When you see them pouring down the hillside, move to the right of the large stone boulder. Doing so draws them between the boulder and the hillside, causing them to bunch up into a large, easy target.

Rush at the large target with your lance, and clean them out of the narrow passage. Your troops should pick up any stragglers that get by.

Leave your men behind and charge the hill just ahead. As you attack the enemies on the hill, their comrades release large boulders to squash you. Dodge the boulders and continue charging up the hill.

Goad the rest of the goblins to draw them out onto the hill. As they rush down at you, the other foolish Goblins release the last two boulders, smashing their own troops.

As before, dash away from the oncoming boulders and continue to attack. The next Goblin commander sits atop the hill—don't let him wait too long.

Stab at him with your lance and drive him back into the surrounding cliff walls. Keep the pressure on him until he succumbs to your might.

Now that the second Goblin commander has fallen, the main gate opens, allowing passage deeper into Fort Wyandeek. Regroup your forces and lead them back down the hill, past the enemy archers.

Make yourself at home and penetrate the main gate as you trek deeper into the Goblin stronghold.

OBJECTIVE
Find and defeat the Orc corporal.

The next area is surrounded by a large hill, which serves as a perfect launching ramp for more Goblins. Just as you pass the gate, the Goblins swarm around you. Set your troops to defend, and don't give the Goblins an inch.

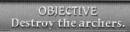

With so many Goblins surrounding you, it is difficult to single out any one particular enemy. Don't try to—use an Orb Attack to cut them down and fill your Orb Spark meter.

Scurry left, across the valley to face the Orc corporal. With your Orb Spark meter full, dash around his troops with your lance stayed. Don't strike at them. First, draw out the rest of the troops from the surrounding hills.

Wait until the rest of his goons are finished coming out of hiding, and rush outside of his troops' ranks. Once outside, turn on the corporal and instantly kill every enemy with an Orb Spark attack. The next gate opens.

OBJECTIVE
Destroy the archers.

Beyond the next gate waits a formidable force. At its front are groups of archers itching to pick off your men. Break their ranks and scatter the enemy archers.

After felling the archers, lead your men west. There you find a young sorceress named Tyurru, who is also protected by the Light.

Though she is holding her own against a troop of villains, aid her in her battle so she can assist you for the rest of your mission.

With Tyurru in tow, march your men to the east side of Fort Wyandeek. Tied to the eastern edge of the canyon is a long, rickety wooden bridge. Unfortunately, it's not strong enough to support all of your troops, so destroy the archers guarding it and turn back to the central valley. The next gate is now open.

OBJECTIVE
Defeat the Orc corporal.

Traipse across the now open gate and aid the dark figure waging war on the Orcs. He is Klarrann, a mysterious priest that is also protected by the Light. Help Klarrann with the Orc corporal and leave your men to handle the surrounding enemies. Finish off the Orc corporal to gain access to the next central gate.

OBJECTIVE
Defeat the Goblin wizards at the altar.

At the final section of Fort Wyandeek, you find something unexpected; these aren't all Goblin soldiers—these are innocent women and children.

Frightened for their lives, they run for the huts along the flanking hills. Let them flee; they are not your target. The attacking Orc squad is.

While Inphyy and her troops dash to the left edge of Fort Wyandeek where the villagers dwell, deactivate your troops and approach the hill alone so as to draw the large boulders. Once all the boulders have been released, return to your guards and regroup. You will need them to attack the main altar.

Lead them past the Goblin reinforcements up to the altar where the priests await. Your squad can be slower than you, so slice past the few groups on the hill leading up to the altar and leave the rest to your squad to clean up.

Before proceeding straight ahead toward the Goblin altar, follow Inphyy and her troops to the village to the left of the central gate. She is driven by a blood rage as she attacks all Goblins in her path.

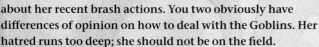

After she slaughters every Goblin she sees, you finally confront her about her recent brash actions. You two obviously have differences of opinion on how to deal with the Goblins. Her hatred runs too deep; she should not be on the field.

Atop the hill, use an Orb Spark to eliminate the wizards' guards. Take out the Troll accompanying the wizards. With their support troops out of the way, focus on the three wizards. Watch for their attack spells and interrupt them before they can turn your troops against you.

Fort Wyandeek falls and a messenger brings word that the Goblin king, Dwykfarrio, fled from Varrgandd to the flatlands. You must hurry, before he advances!

PHOLYA FLATLANDS

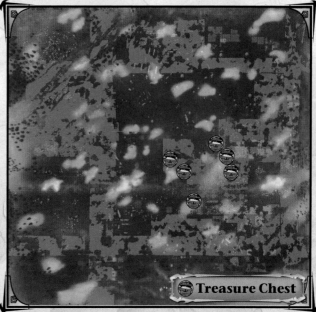

Treasure Chest

The Castle of Varrvazzar has fallen, and Dwykfarrio's Army of Darkness now includes the Outland tribes as they occupy the Pholya Flatlands. The Army of Light has also mustered forces from across the land in preparation for the final battle. But Aspharr is starting to lose sight of why they are fighting in the first place.

**GUARD UNITS
Infantry (x2)**

TIP

Archer guards also work well here. Since the other generals also have their own troops, your archers can stay at a distance and rain arrows on the opposition.

Your infantry marches onto the Pholya Flatlands to do battle with more of Dwykfarrio's Goblin horde. The sides line up on opposite riverbanks and wave their weapons in the air.

Your quest to bring peace back to the land is drawing closer to an end. Dwykfarrio is somewhere on this field. Unfortunately, you need to get past his army to find him.

OBJECTIVE
Destroy the enemy.

Immediately deactivate your infantry and march ahead toward the river. Join the other generals' support guards and leap into the fray. Slash at the enemy grunts and rack up as many Orbs as you can to fill up your gauge.

Dash up and down the riverbanks aiding in battle while your infantry stays rested. Since the battle can get very hectic, work up and down the riverbank to make sure you are helping every general's guards.

After cleaning the battlefield of Goblin fiends, run back to your infantry and reactivate them. Place them in a defensive position and march back to the river.

Orcs have joined the battle on Pholya ground and they now march across the river. Order your forces to take them straight on as you did the Goblins earlier.

These Orcs are tough. Collect Orbs and assault them with an Orb Attack. The bulk of the Orc army can be destroyed here; the rest is a matter of sweeping combos and guard support.

The Arphann return with more dragons under their control. Unless you want to lose more troops to the dragon menace, attack the Arphann without hesitation. Storm across the river and whittle them away with your lance.

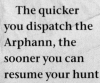

The quicker you dispatch the Arphann, the sooner you can resume your hunt for Dwykfarrio. The dragons come swooping down blowing fire all over the battlefield, so crush the Arphann quickly.

As Dwykfarrio's forces grow, so do yours. Myifee, a mercenary whose blade always comes at a cost, suddenly shows up on the battleground. Has he forsaken his mercenary ways or have truth and justice convinced him to fight for the Light? No matter, his muscle is welcome.

OBJECTIVE
Repel the Orc chieftain, Leuu.

Myifee might be late, but better late than never. Especially now since the Orc chieftain, Leuu, has returned to seek vengeance for his prior defeat.

Take up arms with Leuu. Leave Myifee and his mercenary force to contend with the remaining Goblins, Arphann, or Orcs. Your mission is to stop Leuu, so concentrate on him. Luckily, he has learned little since your last encounter, while you've picked up a few new tricks. Use them on Leuu, or at the very least, use your previous juggle combos on him to take him out of the equation.

Leuu is no match for you, and so he falls a defeated Orc. But before you can get any information out of him, one of Myifee's mercenary companions, Epharr, drives her blade into his gullet.

OBJECTIVE
Defeat Dwingvatt.

As promised, Dwingvatt returns. This time he is backed by Dwykfarrio and even more Goblin reinforcements. Regroup your forces and lead them northeast to face the Goblin leaders.

Make Dwingvatt your own target—you and he have unfinished business. Your men can take

on the Goblin reinforcements just fine. They can hold the Goblins at bay until you, Inphyy, and Myifee finish off Dwingvatt. Once he is down, help your soldiers clean house.

OBJECTIVE
Repel Dwykfarrio.

Dwykfarrio finally decides to meet you face to face. He charges from the northeast with his blades yearning for blood. Your lance, however, seeks only justice and peace.

Scurry up the countryside to take on the Goblin king. Begin by unleashing an Orb attack on him. Use Divine Spear to

launch him backward and chop off bits of his health. Don't let him get up until the Orb charge wears off.

N3 NINETY-NINE NIGHTS

ナインティナイン・ナイツ

PRIMA Official Game Guide

When Dwykfarrio sees your men, he is overcome by the lust for human blood and charges at them almost as if you're not there. When he does, attack him from behind and launch him into the air.

As he lands, charge him again and take more chunks off of his health bar. After a few successful attacks, he is forced to flee one more time.

YWA-UE-UAR FORESTS

Treasure Chest

As the fighting in the Pholya Flatlands comes to a close, the Army of Light drives the Goblin king, Dwykfarrio, into the depths of Ywa-Ue-Uar Forest. Aspharr realizes the reason he fights is to protect those he loves, and he is prepared to die as he sets off to face the Goblin king.

GUARD UNITS
Archers
Infantry

You arrive at the Forbidden Forest in search of Dwykfarrio. He has taken refuge somewhere among the trees and brush, but to bring stability back into the world, hunting him down is a necessary step. If only there were another way.

You order Heppe to guard the rear along with Inphyy. She may not like it, but your decision is final. Besides, it is the only way to keep her at bay and, most importantly, safe.

OBJECTIVE
Find Dwykfarrio.

A group of enemy archers marches directly at you from straight ahead. Sprint ahead to cut them off and set your archers to attack right away. Another group of Dwykfarrio's goons attacks your right flank. Set your infantry to hold them off while you eliminate the first squad.

Return to where you started, make a left, and support your infantry. Both of your squads are essential in this mission, so do everything you can to make sure they survive.

Once all is clear, backtrack to the path leading west and march ahead. Use long chain combos and Orb Attacks to clear the enemies that block your path.

Because the forest paths are full of twists and turns, occasionally stop and let your troops catch up. When you come upon an enemy, be the first to strike and let your archers shower them with arrows from a distance.

Continue marching west until you reach a marshy area. There you will encounter more Goblin resistance. Erase the Goblin horde and follow the path across the marsh as it winds its way north.

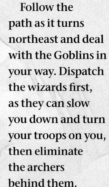

Follow the path as it turns northeast and deal with the Goblins in your way. Dispatch the wizards first, as they can slow you down and turn your troops on you, then eliminate the archers behind them.

As you do, your troops catch up and take little damage. Let the infantry sweep up the archers and your archers stay safely out of harm's way.

The path continues to turn eastward, deeper into the forest. The deeper you get, the more Goblins you must eradicate. Luckily, they attack in small numbers and are easy to eliminate.

OBJECTIVE
Defeat Ppakk.

Turn left up ahead as the path splits and leads west again. Defeat the approaching Orc squad and follow the path northwest this time.

The bend in the road leads directly to Dwykfarrio's kingly companion, Ppakk the Third. He has come again to finish what he started. Welcome him back and finish what *you* started.

Just as before, eliminate his troops with an Orb Attack and leave him to fend for himself. His troops are all bunched in the narrow forest path, so activate your Orb Attack and dash up and down the path until they are all gone.

Once Ppakk stands alone, knock him down with a downward smash of your lance and keep him down. Ppakk is not as fast as smaller enemies, but he is extremely powerful when he connects. So don't let him get up! Keep striking at him on the ground, and knock him back down as he attempts to stand until he perishes at the tip of your lance.

OBJECTIVE
Destroy the unidentified army.

You may have defeated Ppakk, but your quest is far from over. In fact, you are transported deeper into the Forbidden Forest. You find yourself at the forest's far northwest edge, surrounded by a mysterious mist.

You are not alone here, however. Aside from your troops, a mysterious army lies in wait. Its ghastly figures are unlike any humanoid you've ever seen—and they don't seem to happy to see you.

Get to work on them right away. They are tough and fierce opponents. They are swift to crowd around you and attack, but those that can't get within arm's reach send out small silver spheres to attack.

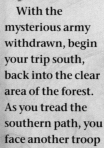

Should any of the spheres burst upon contacting you, they cause major damage and interrupt your flow of attacks. For that reason, attack from above and stay out of the reach of the spheres. Eventually the army withdraws back into the mist.

OBJECTIVE
Destroy the Arphann troop.

With the mysterious army withdrawn, begin your trip south, back into the clear area of the forest. As you tread the southern path, you face another troop of Arphann. Bash them with your lance as your archers pick at them from afar. This fight should not last long, so be quick.

As you defeat the invading Arphann, Syumerrt of the Arff rushes into the fray. His bow and arrow complement your archers as the Arphann crash in around you.

Swing your lance and clear a perimeter around you so as to keep the Arphann from getting too close.

You battle the Arphann in what seems an endless waterfall of enemy forces. Suddenly, the Arphann commander joins the conflict. If you have an Orb Attack, use it against her and send her flying back.

You reach Inphyy just in time to catch her as she falls to the floor, weary from her efforts. As she gets to her feet, she is overwhelmed by emotions and cannot articulate what is in her heart.

Before she can muster up the words, you both sense something strange in the surrounding forest. You take

Chip away at her and back away to defend. She is nimble and extremely fast, so don't use too many leaping attacks that require precise aiming. Instead use large powerful strokes to keep her on the defensive until she falls. When she falls, the Arphann withdraw.

arms, back to back and ready for a fight. Before you get one, though, your men arrive with news of Dwykfarrio's location. He is cornered in the northeast.

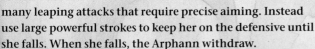

Following the Arphann withdrawal, Heppe comes with news of Inphyy's impulsive actions. It seems that in order to win your approval, she has headed off on her own to hunt Dwykfarrio. Reluctant to go and call her back, Heppe leaves you to do the only thing a brother can do—go rescue his little sister from herself.

Proceed along the path cautiously; Dwykfarrio still has many troops at his command. Before reaching him you must eliminate an Orc troop, a group of Goblins, and another squad of Goblin wizards.

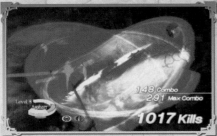

After defeating them all, you reach a small clearing where Dwykfarrio stands defiantly.

Set on the path east as it leads to Dwykfarrio's last known whereabouts and Inphyy's current destination. Defeat the lone enemy group you encounter and press on toward the eastern edge of the forest.

Activate an Orb Attack and rush Dwykfarrio right away. You knock him back and eliminate the last of the troops that stood behind him.

You stop Inphyy from murdering Dwykfarrio and let him scurry into the forest, a frightened beast.

Keep the pressure on as your attacks are charged by the Orb, until the charge runs out. Keep him off balance until reinforcements arrive. Inphyy joins the attack on Dwykfarrio and helps draw attention away from you while knocking him out of his defenses.

While Dwykfarrio escapes, a blinding divine light appears in front of you. Its glow is radiant and calming. Is this the divine Light approving of your noble deeds? Perhaps it's a symbol of peace returning to the land....

Your joint efforts best Dwykfarrio. Defeated, alone, and humiliated, the Goblin king is at the mercy of your lance. He stares up at you not knowing his fate.

Inphyy rushes at him one more time, hoping to drive her blade into him, to finish things once and for all. She seeks vengeance for your father's death, but your goal is much nobler. The Goblin king is defeated, so peace will once again grace your lands.

Age:
32
Class:
Warrior
Weapon:
Twin-Bladed Sword
Orb Spark:
Fire

Myifee appears carefree, but in reality, he's skilled and serious. Born into a long line of lawyers and officials, he chooses instead to live as a mercenary, saving those oppressed by war. He uses a dual-bladed sword.

Growing up around lawyers gave him a shrewd insight into Human nature. He disguises his disillusionment behind a flippant demeanor. Acting on the spur of the moment, he joined the mercenary unit hoping to catch the lovely Epharr's eye.

VITAL STATISTICS

Category	Level 1	Level 2	Level 3	Level 4	Level 5	Level 6	Level 7	Level 8	Level 9
Default Attack Point	100	110	121	133	146	161	177	195	214
Default HP	1,100	1,460	2,112	3,626	4,220	5,500	8,800	14,266	22,108
Default Defense Point	20	22	24	27	29	32	35	39	43
Default Rate of Critical Hit	10	11	12	12	13	13	14	15	16

COMBO ATTACKS

Myifee's fighting style is perfectly suited to him: fiery, powerful, and very over-the-top. His blades are attached to a chain that he uses to pull them back after launching them at enemies. Like a large, dangerous yo-yo, Myifee's swords are lethal in his possession.

Level 1

Myifee's level 1 combos take some getting used to. Less-experienced players might have a hard time staying alive at first. His dual-bladed sword flies out of his hand in large circular strikes, leaving the area nearest to Myifee exposed.

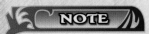

> **NOTE**
>
> When doing a combo attack, execute button presses separated by commas in quick succession.
>   If the move says ", then" or ", press", allow the final move to finish before pressing the next button command.

Move	Execution
Brave Swing	X, X, X, X, Y
Bull Fireball	During Orb Attack, press X
Burst Slash	In mid-dash, press X (or Y)
Double Deathscythe	X, X, Y, Y
Double Hand Flame	X, X, X, Y
Flame Back Knuckle	X, Y
Flying Edge	In mid-jump, press X
Howling Flame	Y, Y, Y, X, X repeatedly, then press X
Man on Fire	X, X, X, X
Max Volcano	During Orb Attack, press Y
Round Swing	Y, X

Level 2

Level 2 combos introduce two of Myifee's most impressive moves, Destroyer Throw and Deadly Throw. With them you can hurl impaled enemies at their brethren.

Move	Execution
Calling Terror	Y, Y, X
Deadly Throw	While stabbing an enemy, press Y
Death Down Head	Y, X, X
Destroyer Throw	While stabbing an enemy, press X
Flame Run	Y, Y, Y, Y
Flame Slash	X, X, X, X, X
Myifee's Rage	X, X, X, Y, Y

Level 3

At level 3, Myifee's combo list gains various long-chain attack combos good for keeping enemies on the defensive. One level 3 move, Myifee Dynamite, is very successful against midsize boss enemies.

Move	Execution
Dancing Wiz Flame	X, X, X, X, X, X
Deadly Typhoon	X, Y, X
Myifee Dynamite	In mid-jump, press Y
Raging Bull	X, X, X, X, Y, Y
Triple Deathscythe	X, X, Y, Y, Y

Level 4

One of the level 4 moves, Charging Bull, is the first of a few combos that drain Orb energy. Use Charging Bull sparingly, because an Orb Attack can be more effective when needed.

Move	Execution
Charging Bull	Y, Y, Y, X, X, then Y (drains Orb Attack gauge)
Deathscythe Dawn	X, X, Y, Y, Y, Y

Level 5

Myifee learns one of his easiest, yet most useful combo attacks at level 5: Final Slash. This combo is just as it sounds: a series of slashes that is the last thing an enemy ever sees.

Move	Execution
Final Slash	X, X, X, X, X, X, X
Volcano	X, X, X, Y, Y, Y

Level 6

Level 6 introduces one move. However, it is one of Myifee's very few aerial maneuvers. Because of his brute strength and heavy weight, Myifee will oftentimes be surrounded by enemies. In those situations, moves like Flying Deathscythe are crucial.

Move	Execution
Flying Deathscythe	In mid-jump, press X

Level 7

Myifee's level 7 move is dangerous. Aptly named Hellfire, it burns up his opponents.

Move	Execution
Hellfire	X, X, X, Y, Y, Y

Level 8

Another of the Orb Attack gauge-draining moves, level 8's Inferno is just as dangerous as Hellfire. Use it sparingly, though; you will always need Orb energy.

Move	Execution
Inferno	✗,✗,✗,✓,✓,✓,✗ (drains Orb Attack gauge)

Level 9

This is Myifee's final and possibly most devastating move. Bull's Fury is just as it sounds, a furious attack that crushes nearby enemies almost instantly.

Move	Execution
Bull's Fury	✗,✗,✓,✓,✓,✗ (drains Orb Attack gauge)

WEAPONS

Myifee's unique weapons are an odd mix of deadly design and playful execution. Since his dual-bladed swords are essentially two swords attached at the hilts, they deal massive damage with just one swing. Additionally, because they are attached to a chain, they can be tossed great distances, reaching enemies farther away, and brought back like a boomerang.

Double Edge

Level 1

A sharp, double-sided sword with a chain, the Double Edge is Myifee's default weapon.

Double Sword

Level 2

Forged by a skilled blacksmith of great swords, this weapon increases Attack range by 15 percent and critical rate by 10 percent.

Tornado

Level 3

Tornado is a powerful weapon that emits flames at extreme speeds. It increases Attack power by 10 percent, Attack range by 20 percent, and Defense power by 25 percent.

Dual Crescent

Level 4

This sword follows an elegant arc as it slices. It boosts Attack power 20 percent, Attack range 30 percent, and critical rate 20 percent.

Tempest

Level 5

A hellish sword that wreaks pure havoc, Tempest increases Attack power and critical rate by 60 percent and Attack range by 50 percent; all critical damage is avoided.

Black Ox

Level 6

A double sword also known as "Big Bull," this weapon increases Attack power 40 percent, Attack range 40 percent, and Defense power 20 percent.

Ansalar

Level 7

This magic sword has a mind of its own. Luckily, its effects show an increase of 50 percent in Attack power and Attack range, and 30 percent increases in Speed, Orb appear rate, and Orb Attack length.

Weapon Locations and Conditions

Weapon	Location/Condition
Double Edge	Default weapon
Double Sword	Rescue two villagers in Felppe Village and open the treasure chest behind the church
Tornado	Treasure chest in Varrgandd Castle
Dual Crescent	Treasure chest in Ice Gate Mission
Black Ox	Treasure chest in Everr Mountains Mission
Ansalar	Treasure chest in Pholya Mission
Tempest	Found during Tea Tea's cutscene in Vargandd

LOVE AND WAR

Myifee is a skilled warrior and a very successful mercenary. However, his recent dealings as a mercenary have led him to believe that there is no longer worthy profit to be made in war. Sure, there is good money, but at the continued risk of his own neck? No reward is *that* good.

One day, as he relaxes outside the mercenary offices, his feet kicked up, arms comfortably folded behind his head, a mysterious figure inquires about where one can sign up as a merc. It's Epharr, a dark and brooding female warrior whose enthusiasm for war borders on bloodlust. Intrigued by her determination, Myifee also signs up.

FELPPE VILLAGE

Treasure Chest

Myifee realizes that this battle could be his last, but he joins the mercenaries anyway. As the battle intensifies, Myifee becomes key to the success and survival of the Army of Light.

Led by Captain Badokk, you, Epharr, and the rest of the mercenary troops calmly march to Felppe Village. The village has come under attack by Orc invaders, and its citizens cry out for help.

Up ahead, a little girl scrambles for her life. As soon as Epharr hears of the Orc presence, she storms off into the village to bathe her blade in Orc blood.

OBJECTIVE
Defeat the Orcs and rescue the girl.

Walk up to the Orc invaders attacking the girl by the well and let them pick on someone their own size...or slightly smaller. Reach the little girl and use your blades to form a perimeter around her.

After you clear the Orc force out of the well area, the little girl informs you that there are more villagers trapped in the church atop the village's hill. Her mother is one of the people trapped.

Mommy's in the church.

OBJECTIVE
To the church, quickly!

Run up the main village road to the church. As you approach, eliminate the six groups of Orcs attacking the houses lining the village street.

Lunging up the hill allows you to catch them from behind, granting you the element of surprise. Take them down with your sword and absorb their Orbs.

You reach the church to find a helpless woman cowering in front of the church, surrounded by angry Orcs. Do to them what you did to their brethren and rescue the poor woman.

As mother and daughter reunite, three Orc battalions converge on the church.

OBJECTIVE
Destroy the Orcs surrounding the church.

Let the three Orc swarms converge around you as the woman and her daughter escape. The Orcs mean business; luckily, being a mercenary, you are just what they need—a businessman.

As they crowd you, roll out of the murderous mess until you are beyond their reach. When they stream toward you, turn around and unleash an Orb Attack.

Orc bodies lie strewn around your feet like last night's empty bottles, and your blade begins to glisten. It's not glistening from blood, however; this is a magical glow.

The air swirls around you, and a light swallows you whole. You are the newest recipient of the protection of the Light. With your Orb Spark meter now full, you can execute an Orb Spark attack!

Unimpressed by your newfound power, Captain Badokk scorns you for leaving your group behind to rescue the villagers at the church. You explain that you got carried away, but he is not easily soothed.

Then, a messenger arrives with startling news. The enemy has laid siege on Varrgandd, and the attack on Felppe Village was just a distraction. They will not get away with this!

OBJECTIVE
Destroy the Orcs.

Just east of the village hill where the church sits, Epharr is surrounded by four Orc squads. Rush down the hill and play "knight in shining armor."

She may be tough as nails, but even she needs help from time to time. Besides, this is an excellent opportunity to test out your new attack. Just before you find yourself surrounded by Orcs, stop and unleash the Orb Spark.

BASTIDE OF VARRGANDD

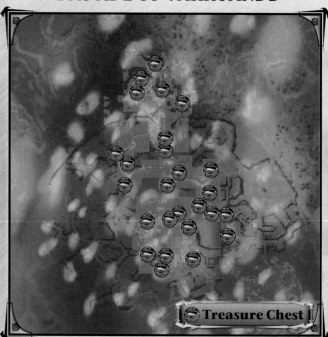

Treasure Chest

With the protection of the light, Myifee easily defeats the Orc raid on Felppe Village. But that is just a diversion, as at the moment, the Bastide of Varrgandd is also under attack from Goblin forces and their catapults.

GUARD UNITS
Infantry
Heavy Infantry

You arrive at Varrgandd just in time to see it overrun with Goblins. Its walls are being peppered by catapults, and the ground forces are on the verge of defeat. Only you and your mercenaries can turn the tide!

OBJECTIVE
Destroy the Goblin troops.

After the catapults fall, turn your attention on the ground troops behind you. If they go unchecked, they can overtake your mercenary forces.

Show them your mercenary strength and streak across their ranks like a comet. Let your blades propel you across the field until the Goblin horde is nothing more than stains upon the grass.

OBJECTIVE
Destroy all the catapults before the wall collapses.

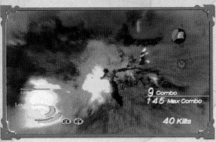

The catapults assaulting the walls are just beyond the forest edge, at the base of two small hillocks. Set your troops to defend and lead them past the invading Goblin troops.

Your main priority is the wall. Get to the catapults and destroy them. Search the surrounding area for chests with Orb containers and fill your Orb Attack gauge. Once full, let loose on the catapults.

OBJECTIVE
Destroy the Goblins attacking the North Gate.

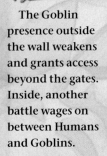

The Goblin presence outside the wall weakens and grants access beyond the gates. Inside, another battle wages on between Humans and Goblins.

The North Gate is about to fall, unless you do something about it. Take arms against the Goblin horde and chop them down until the North Gate is once again secure.

NOTE

Sweep the area in the blinking square on the map to make sure you get every last Goblin.

The North Gate is saved, but the East Gate falls. Orcs burst into Varrgandd brandishing their weapons as they thirst for Human blood.

Epharr leaps into action and gives chase to the Orc commanders. Every time an Orc surfaces, she is the first to raise her blade. Follow her to give her support.

With the castle Orc-less, a soldier arrives with news of sorceress Tyurru's battle with the Orc at the South Gate. Head south toward the next gate to provide her with aid.

On your way there, you trample on a would-be thief as he ponders his next five-finger discount. The rascal's name is Tea Tea, and he doesn't take well to you sneaking up on him. Tea Tea draws his sword and boldly challenges you to a fight. Oblige him.

OBJECTIVE
Destroy the Orcs inside the castle!

Streak south along the castle avenues past the marketplace and face the invading Orc. There are various adjacent paths along the castle interior, and all are filled with enemies.

Back away from intersections in the castle paths and draw the enemies into the narrow confines of a single street. As they file in, launch yourself into their midst and pummel them. Continue street sweeping until the castle is Orc-free.

Tea Tea is an impressive combatant indeed. Let your support troops distract him by engaging him in combat. Meanwhile, back away and round the fight until Tea Tea has his back to you.

After he lunges at one of your soldiers, strike at his back. Knock him to the floor and keep him off his feet. He is extremely quick, so use small combos to chip away at his health. If you use long sweeps and combos, you leave yourself open to a counterattack.

Continue to chip away at him until he drops to his knees and begs for mercy. As you stand over him with your blades in your hand, he offers to do anything if you spare his life.

Needing help in the war effort, you spare his life as long as he joins your mercenary crew. He is reluctant at first but caves in and picks up his sword. Tea Tea joins your mercenary squad.

Resume your trek to the southern end of the castle to defend against the encroaching Orcs. As you rush to the rescue, you come across more Goblin resistance. Wipe them out lest they follow you to the Orc encampment.

OBJECTIVE
Destroy the Orc elite units.

Just outside the castle walls, a large group of Orc elite units has amassed. It's your responsibility to eliminate them.

Rush out and meet them head on. If you have an Orb Attack available, use it right away. Eliminate the Orc chieftains' squads and leave the three elite commanders standing alone.

More Goblin reinforcements arrive to aid the Orc cause. As they do, let your troops tie them up while you single out one of the Orc chieftains.

After discarding the first chieftain, turn your attention to the other two. Single them out, one by one, by keeping on the heavy offensive until they are all dead.

When all three chieftains fall, the rest of the Orcs retreat. Let them escape; the castle is safe. More news arrives about the enemy's march on the Castle of Varrvazzar while the Goblin presence in Fort Wyandeek readies to mobilize.

Tyurru dashes up to Fort Wyandeek while you gather your forces and prepare to aid the people of Varrvazzar.

ICE GATE

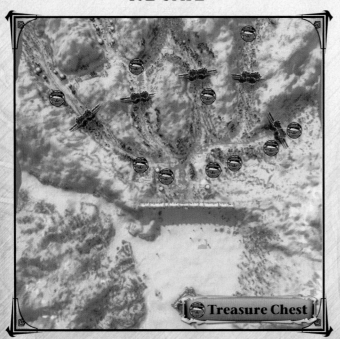

Treasure Chest

Varrgandd is a saved, thanks to the heroic and frenzied efforts of the mercenaries. But they soon learn that war is accelerating. With his new pal Tea Tea, Myifee heads through the snowy landscape to the castle at Varrgandd, only to find it and the Ice Gate on the brink of falling to the Orc army.

**GUARD UNITS
Heavy Infantry
Archers**

You tread the icy path to the Castle of Varrvazzar with your mercenaries right behind you. Epharr's gait is hurried and eager, while Badokk walks cautiously as if always on the lookout. You can't help but wonder what it is that drives Epharr so passionately.

**OBJECTIVE
Rescue Vyarrhertenn.**

One of the castle's gates, Gate Two, is just ahead, and Vyarrhertenn wages battle on its other side. The gate is about to fall unless you help out.

Leave the castle and help Vyarrhertenn out. Stay near him to make sure he doesn't take too much damage while you chop down the Orcs outside the castle gate. Sweep both sides of the gate clean of all Orcs and the gate is rescued.

**OBJECTIVES
Rescue Vyden.
Defeat the Gewg chieftain.**

After sealing Gate Two, scurry over to Gate One, where Vyden is making a valiant stand against more incoming Orcs. To make matters worse, a force of Gewgs joins the battle.

Welcome the Gewg chieftain to the fight by spinning your blades in his scaly face. Two or three strong combos and the Gewg chieftain falls to your blade as well, thus sealing Gate One. Stay near Vyden to ensure his safety, just as you did Vyarrhertenn's.

OBJECTIVES
Rescue Vyertenn.
Defeat the Arphann chieftain Pyurrott.

OBJECTIVES
Rescue Vyertenn.
Defeat the Arphann chieftain Pyurrott.

Another battle rages on ahead. Vyertenn also valiantly defends the castle from invading enemies. This time, however, he is on the brink of losing the battle. He faces battles on two fronts; one with the Gewg and another against the Arphann.

Relieve him of the Arphann chieftain by eliminating her from the equation. She is extremely dangerous, so approach this fight the same way you approached Tea Tea; attack her from behind while she is distracted. When the chieftain is defeated, the threat of a dragon invasion is no more.

CAUTION

The Arphann chieftain has many fast and powerful combo attacks capable of chopping more than one-quarter of a health bar at once.

OBJECTIVE
Rescue the wounded Lord Vyden.

Proceed south to aid the wounded Lord Vyden. Dash past the enemies strewn about the icy ground and finish off any enemies that still remain.

When you arrive at Lord Vyden's location he lies wounded on the ground. Tea Tea rushes to his side. Reunited with his estranged father, Tea Tea vows to continue helping seal the Ice Gate.

OBJECTIVE
Destroy the invading enemy.

Dart over to the Ice Gate along the eastern path outside the castle. There you collide with a massive army of enemies led by two Trolls.

Don't whittle away at the constant stream of enemies; instead focus your attacks on the two Trolls. As they fall, the Arphann, Gewg, and Pwuck all continually crash down around you. Stand your ground and use Orb Attacks as frequently as possible.

After you fell the entire invading force, word comes of Dwykfarrio's advance on the Pholya Flatlands. He marches there to gather his Outland forces and prepare a strike on the Humans.

Though Tea Tea has held up his end of the deal you made, he promises to continue helping out. It's off to the Pholya Flatlands!

EVERR MOUNTAINS

Treasure Chest

Lead your troops south to surprise the Goblins as they wait. Your numbers are greater and capable of squashing the small squadron up ahead with ease. Charge down the path and destroy every last Goblin.

The Army of Darkness that felled the Ice Gate is gathering in the Pholya Flatlands, and the Army of Light is en route to the flatlands as well. Meanwhile, Myifee and the mercenaries wait for the Arphann marching toward Pholya in the Everr Mountains.

**GUARD UNITS
Heavy Infantry
(x2)**

OBJECTIVE
Overrun the Goblin positions.

Just below the Everr Mountains, you gather your forces and await the enemy's approach. Your troops are blood-soaked, weary, and yet still very eager to trim the fat off the enemy flanks.

As you stand there, catching your icy breath, you spy Goblins just south of your position. They are gathered in small bunches, ripe for the picking.

This is the place. The Arrphan will pass with their dragons. We'll attack them from here!

This is the place. The Arrphan will pass with their dragons. We'll attack them from here!

OBJECTIVE
Destroy the enemy.

Eradicate the Goblins atop the hill and continue down until more enemy squads appear. Hold them off until your archer support arrives.

As you hold off the initial troops, more enemies attack from the branching paths to the south. Stand your ground until the Arphann arrive with their dragons in tow.

Round up your mercenaries and get moving! Crash into the Arphann like a wave of steel meeting soft flesh. Carve through them with your blades while your troops finish off what you don't.

If you have an Orb Attack, use it against the dragon masters. The first wave falls and another approaches from behind.

Behind you, more dragon-toting Arphann approach. Turn around and deliver the same fate to them as you did their Arphann sisters.

In what seems to be a last ditch effort, the enemy forces stream in from the north and south to pinch you in. The forces from the north are less; take them out first. Then eliminate the enemies from the south.

Use an Orb Attack to drop the Arphann and the dragons, and chop a huge chunk of the Troll's health off. When the Troll is the last enemy standing, regroup your forces and swarm him. He is the last to stand on Everr Mountains. Next stop, the Pholya Flatlands.

PHOLYA FLATLANDS

⊙ Treasure Chest

The mercenaries successfully stop the Arphann in the Everr Mountains, but back at the Pholya Flatlands, full-scale war has broken out between the forces of Dark and Light. Everything will come down to this one moment in the flatlands, where fate will take its course.

GUARD UNITS
Heavy Infantry
Archers

OBJECTIVE
Rescue the Temple Knights.

The mercenaries set foot on the flatlands as the Temple Knights engage the Goblin horde. Inphyy fights furiously on the field as waves of Goblins crash all around her.

The Temple Knights are under attack, and though you are late, they are happy to see you. Set your troops to defend and rush past the first few enemy troops to aid the Temple Knights in the west.

Don't worry about the enemy squads you just passed up; they will get their due. The important thing is to rescue the Temple Knights and secure their survival so that Inphyy has backup when meeting Dwykfarrio.

Enemies will attempt to funnel in through the bridge, and you are the only one that can clog it. Stay on or behind the bridge, but not in front of it. As enemies funnel into the narrow bridge passage, let your swords fly. If any enemies get by, your troops take care of them.

Make a stand on the bridge and don't allow any enemies to get by. Watch the Block Rate counter atop the screen and keep your numbers high.

OBJECTIVE
Destroy the enemy.

Once rescued, the Temple Knights continue to demolish the Goblin horde. At this rate the enemy will fall. However, reinforcements are on their way from the north. Burn past the enemy on your way up to the reinforcements.

Stay on the offensive to keep the Block Rate counter above 50. If the counter dips below 40, let an Orb Attack fly.

Your stand on the bridge works and the enemy reinforcements are pushed back. Unfortunately, Epharr finds herself in danger in the east.

Fall back and make a mad dash east to rescue her. Oddly enough, a thick mist hides the path east. No matter—Epharr needs you. Press on until you find a bridge hidden in the mist.

OBJECTIVE
Intercept the enemy reinforcements.

Dash north to the small bridge. Set your troops to defend to ensure they follow you to the bridge. Once there, take a position at the middle of the bridge.

OBJECTIVE
Defeat VigkVagk.

On the other side of the bridge, a nefarious Troll, VigkVagk, assaults Epharr and her troops. Rush to her aid and take aim at VigkVagk's battalion.

Use an Orb Attack to kill off his group. With them out of the way, turn your attention on the speedy Troll leader. VigkVagk is unlike any other Troll you have faced thus far. He is fast, he is agile, and he is strategic.

Stay out of reach from VigkVagk's downward smash attack and group with Epharr to inflict major damage on the Troll. Your troops aren't as effective as before, as VigkVagk focuses his anger on you.

Stay on the move and combine efforts with Epharr to bring down the overgrown goon. In the end, you stand back to back with Epharr, panting amidst the enemy remains. Before long, Epharr once again jumps into a sprint and runs off.

OBJECTIVE
Defeat Orc chieftain Leuu.

Follow Epharr into the mist-covered area to the east. There she faces off against the incoming Orc invaders led by Leuu.

Take out his Orc reinforcements while Epharr goes to work on the Orc chieftain. After clearing out his troops, join Epharr in chopping down the large chieftain tree. Between the two of you, he falls quickly.

Leuu is defeated, and you prepare to deliver the final blow. However, as you lift your blades in the air, Epharr rushes in and sticks her blade in Leuu, robbing him of his final breath.

She reveals that she was once an Orc slave and was robbed of her childhood. Having robbed Leuu of his life, she sits there tired, her vengeance fulfilled. You comfort her and reassure her that it is all over. Finally, you two can begin a life together. Perhaps this new life can fill the empty hole the Orcs left.

DWINGVATT'S QUEST

Age:
15

Class:
Soldier

Weapon:
Dual Sword

Orb Spark:
Wind

A proud Goblin soldier, Dwingvatt curses his Human-like skin. His older brother was killed in front of him by a female Human knight. One of Dwingvatt's swords is a memento of his slain brother.

Protected by his big brother during hard times, he was bright and friendly. But when his beloved brother Dwinga was killed by a Human knight, he gained an extraordinary desire to destroy those who took Dwinga.

VITAL STATISTICS

Category	Level 1	Level 2	Level 3	Level 4	Level 5	Level 6	Level 7	Level 8	Level 9
Default Attack Point	100	110	121	133	146	161	177	195	214
Default HP	1,000	1,400	2,236	3,226	4,196	5,300	8,600	13,256	21,428
Default Defense Point	20	22	24	27	29	32	35	39	43
Default Rate of Critical Hit	10	11	12	13	14	15	16	17	18

COMBO ATTACKS

Dwingvatt's fighting style is fast and furious. Just as his profile describes, Dwingvatt is consumed by an "extraordinary desire to destroy those who took Dwinga." His desire to avenge his brother translates into a powerful attack style composed of extremely fast combos with multiple, almost indiscernible strikes.

Level 1

Dwingvatt has low HP and attack points, so make good use of his finishing moves to defeat enemies. Because his moves are very fast and have virtually no delay, he does not get hit easily. Dwingvatt should never be stuck in the middle of enemies, however, especially if they are bosses. Use his escaping skills to get behind them. Most of his moves bring his enemies' guard down and have high chances for critical damage. Take advantage of this even further by equipping items that enhance these traits.

NOTE

When doing a combo attack, execute button presses separated by commas in quick succession.

If the move says ", then" or ", press", allow the final move to finish before pressing the next button command.

Move	Execution
Blade	❌,❌,❌,❌,❌
Brink	ⓇⓉ, then press ❌
Cruelty	❌,❌
Disorder	During Orb Attack, press ❌
Faithful	❌,❌,❌,❌
Flash	❌,❌,❌,❌,❌
Fly	During headstomp, press ❌
Justice	❌,❌,❌
Pound	❌,❌,❌
Remorse	❌,❌,❌,❌
Sky	In mid-jump, press ❌
Small	In mid-jump, press ❌, land, then press ❌
Soft	In mid-jump, press ❌
Zenith	During Orb Attack, press ❌

Level 2

At level 2, Dwingvatt gains a host of useful combo attacks. Attacks like Chase will become a staple for Dwingvatt players.

Move	Execution
Bind	❌,❌,❌,❌
Blaze	❌,❌,❌,❌
Chase	❌,❌,❌,❌,❌,❌,❌
Cross	During headstomp, press ❌
Erupt	ⓇⓉ, then press ❌

Level 3

Moves like Dig and Sense increase Dwingvatt's ability to cause damage. All combos are fast and most effective when executed at close range.

Move	Execution
Chaos	❌,❌,❌,❌,❌
Dig	❌,❌,❌,❌,❌,❌,❌
Fang	During headstomp, press ❌
Phosphorus	❌,❌,❌,❌,❌
Poke	ⓇⓉ, then press ❌,❌
Sense	❌,❌,❌,❌,❌,❌
Swallow	❌,❌,❌,❌,❌,❌
Tension	❌,❌,❌,❌,❌
Trial	❌,❌,❌,❌,❌

Level 4

Level 4's Hate attack is best used sparingly. Because it drains the Orb Attack gauge, its usefulness is limited to moments of extreme need.

Move	Execution
Defy	ⓇⓉ, then press ❌,❌,❌
Hate	❌,❌,❌,❌,❌,❌,❌,❌,❌ (drains Orb Attack gauge)
Pierce	❌,❌,❌,❌,❌,❌,❌

Level 5

Temper is one of Dwingvatt's easiest moves to pull off. In keeping with his style, it is fast and easy to recover from should it not completely connect.

Move	Execution
Grief	❌,❌,❌,❌,❌ (drains Orb Attack gauge)
Storm	❌,❌,❌,❌,❌,❌
Temper	❌,❌,❌,❌,❌,❌,❌,❌,❌,❌

Level 6

The epitome of Dwingvatt's style, the Shade move caps off a combo chain in dazzling fashion.

Move	Execution
Shade	Ⓧ,Ⓧ,Ⓧ,Ⓧ,Ⓨ,Ⓨ,Ⓨ,Ⓨ,Ⓨ

Level 7

Although the move gained at level 7 is named Trust, no one but Dwingvatt should trust this move. It is short but deadly.

Move	Execution
Trust	Ⓨ,Ⓨ,Ⓧ,Ⓨ,Ⓧ

Level 8

Perhaps it is not anger that fuels Dwingvatt, but woe. Regardless, this Woe is a great combo attack to use on bosses.

Move	Execution
Woe	Ⓨ,Ⓨ,Ⓧ,Ⓧ,Ⓨ

WEAPONS

Dwingvatt's dual swords are perfect for dealing damage quickly and efficiently. Because they are small swords attached to his arms, they strike as if he was attacking with his fists. No heavy swords to swing, no over-sized scepters with a slow recovery rate, no blades attached to chains like yo-yos; Dwingvatt's dual swords are the perfect weapons for a fast and furious combat.

Twin Fang

Level 1

Twin Fang is a dagger left to Dwingvatt by his brother Dwinga. This is Dwingvatt's default weapon.

Assassin's Dagger

Level 2

The Assassin's Dagger is lightweight and easy to handle. Critical rate increases 20 percent when this weapon is equipped.

Deviltooth

Level 3

A legendary dagger with thorn-like ornaments, Deviltooth increases Attack power by 40 percent, Attack range by 80 percent, Speed by 20 percent, and Orb charge speed by 50 percent.

Khukuri

Level 3

Khukuri is a dagger with a unique contour. Attack power rises by 20 percent, Attack range goes up 20 percent, and critical rate increases by 10 percent.

Black Scimitar

Level 4

The divine dagger of an Orb protector, Black Scimitar enhances Attack power by 40 percent and Attack range by 30 percent.

Nemesis

Level 5

Nemesis is a dagger of hatred filled with the power to kill Humans. Attack power increases by 40 percent, Defense power goes up 50 percent, and critical rate rises by 50 percent.

Hell's Dagger

Level 6

This dagger of madness steals life and brings death. It increases Attack range by 50 percent, critical rate by 100 percent, and Guard break rate by 50 percent.

Weapon Locations and Conditions

Weapon	Location/Condition
Twin Fang	Default weapon
Assassin's Dagger	Treasure chest in Varrgandd Mission
Khukuri	Treasure chest in Varrgandd Mission
Black Scimitar	Treasure chest in Ice Gate Mission
Nemesis	Treasure chest in Varrvazarr Mission
Hell's Dagger	Treasure chest in Pholya Mission
Deviltooth	Destroy a specific tower in Ice Gate Mission

A BROTHER'S LOVE, A GOBLIN'S HATE

The day started off like any other. Goblins were going about their business around the village and everything seemed normal in spite of the rumors of war. Word had begun to spread that the Humans were on the rampage and wanted something called "Orb." Suddenly, a Goblin messenger finds his way back to the village, in spite of an injury.

Humans are marching toward the village and they can't be stopped. Dwinga tosses his little brother Dwingvatt into a nearby hut and runs off to protect the village from the incoming Humans. As Dwingvatt peers out of the hut's cracks in terror, he sees a female knight, clad in red, drive her blade into Dwinga's back as he protects an innocent mother and child. The day that had started off like any other ended with a seed of hatred planted in Dwingvatt's heart.

BASTIDE OF VARRGANDD

 Treasure Chest

Countless battles had been fought between the Humans and Goblins. But this battle is different. Dwykfarrio's speech about a new world where Goblins could live in peace hits the core of Goblins everywhere. Dwingvatt swears vengeance against the Humans for the murder of his brother Dwinga and joins the initial assault on Varrgandd.

The troops rally outside of Varrgandd castle as King Dwykfarrio's army prepares to fell the kingdom of Humans. The king plans to unite the two halves of the Orb and bring peace to the Goblin nation.

But for that to happen the Humans must be made to pay for what they have done, and they must hand over the Orb of Light. They aren't going to comply, so it's up to you to force their hand. Your journey begins here.

NOTE

Because Dwingvatt is a soldier, he does not command troops in battle.

NOTE

Don't bother attempting to flank the enemy on your initial charge; the ways to the left and right are both blocked.

OBJECTIVE
Defeat the captain of the Varrgandd defenders.

As the soldiers around you rush in and take up arms against the Humans, use your uncanny speed to dash past all skirmishes. Your priority is the captain of the defenders. Streak past all Human enemies on your way to the captain, and stop only to occasionally fill your Orb Attack gauge.

The captain is deep behind enemy lines, but your speed makes you a difficult target. Once you have filled up the Orb Attack gauge, strike the captain and unleash an Orb Attack on his troops. Finish him off once he is the last Human standing.

OBJECTIVE
Defeat Myifee the mercenary.
Destroy the enemy to increase the mission success rate.

The filthy Human captain is your first victim, but soon another Human arrives from the north: Myifee, the mercenary, marches in to Varrgandd castle hoping to help his fellow man.

Sprint deeper into the castle, dashing northwest, to meet and kill the mercenary. As you wend your way toward him, kill as many guilty Humans as possible. The more you kill, the more Orbs you gather, and the higher the success rate is for your mission.

Wage war on Myifee—he is no better than the red knight who killed your brother. A Human is a Human, and they are all responsible for his death! As you fight your way deeper into the castle, the other Goblin soldiers penetrate the castle walls.

Let them take on Myifee's men, while you single him out and slice him up. He is a skilled combatant, so wait until he stops blocking before you strike. If you approach him head on, he will block the majority of your attacks, so flank him as much as possible; you're faster than he is.

Block his attacks in return and dash away from the attacks that you cannot block. His weapon can reach far, but your dash can get you out of its range.

As he winds down with a combo attack, sneak up behind him and chip away at his health. Eventually your hit-and-run tactics prove too much for the overgrown Human and he falls.

OBJECTIVE
Defeat the gate keeper and open the castle gates.

Leave Myifee defeated behind you as you take on your next mission objective. More of your brethren wait outside the castle gates, yet there is no way for them to penetrate the walls.

Run southeast along the castle avenues to reach the castle gate. Along the way, continue to eliminate Humans to ensure the mission succeeds, but don't make it your top priority. Right now, opening the gate is of the utmost importance.

Locate the captain of the guards amidst a mess of vile men. He is the key to opening the gate. Assault him with multiple combos, too fast for him to defend against, and let your fellow soldiers penetrate the gate.

OBJECTIVES
Defeat Klarrann and the Varrgandd castellan, Ugort.

Behind the now-open gates stand Klarrann and Ugort, the castellan. Of the two, Klarrann is more powerful. Rather than take on the two at once, dash right, swing around the castle pillars, and get behind Klarrann.

Attack Ugort first, while Klarrann calmly walks up to the battle. Klarrann's overconfidence will be Ugort's downfall as your combo attacks are much too speedy for him to defend against. Klarrann cannot arrive in time to defend Ugort, and Ugort dies.

With Ugort down, take a moment to clear the battleground of other Human interlopers. Use an Orb Attack to finish off the surrounding Humans, as they can get in the way of your fight with Klarrann.

Block as Klarrann assaults you with his giant scepter, and wait for the swings of his weapon to expose a weakness. When that happens, immediately strike him down to the ground. As he gets up, jump up and come down on him with a follow-up attack.

Dash around your slower enemy, striking as you go. When he slams his scepter down upon the ground, streak away from the attack and catch him from behind. After your endless barrage of attacks the Human is defeated.

Your quest to avenge Dwinga has begun. Hopefully your brother is watching from above.

The Ice Gates are breached, and your soldiers march in. The Goblins will take over the castle of Varrgandd! This fight is for the Outlands borders.

OBJECTIVE
Help your allies breach the gates.

In order to breach the gate, help your fellow soldiers whittle down the defenses. The gate is 200 Humans strong, so reducing their numbers will be tough. Watch the Gate Endurance counter atop the screen to keep track of how many Humans you need to eliminate for the gate to fall.

ICE GATE

Treasure Chest

There's no time to revel in the victory at Varrgandd—you're off to the next destination, the Ice Gate. A product of mankind's overconfident ego, it towers high on the tundra. The Outlands tribes have converged, now united and marching toward freedom and liberation, and away from years of oppression. The Ice Gate must fall, at any cost.

When the counter falls to less than 60, Vyarrhertenn joins the battle and attempts to reinforce his troops. Use fast combos to get him outside the skirmish and face him one on one. There you can eliminate him quickly and force the troops to withdraw.

As the gate falls, Orc support attacks Gate Two to the east. Leave your position at Gate One and run over to help the Orcs break through the next gate.

Just as before, a Gate Endurance counter pops up atop your screen. Help the Orcs endure 200 Humans, and as you approach 60 on the counter, Vyden shows up itching for a fight.

Finish off the remaining troops and single out Vydenn. Any Orcs that remain help take on Vydenn and provide much-welcome backup. Just before his health bar diminishes to zero, Vydenn retreats, leaving Gate Two to fall.

At Gate Three, the Arphann begin their assault. Sprint east to reach the third gate and lend the Arphann a helping hand. Upon your arrival, Pyurrott, the Arphann chieftain, welcomes you to the battle.

Help her out and eliminate another 200 Humans until

Vyertenn arrives. When he does, pin him against a nearby wall or hillside and pummel him with endless combos until he retreats.

OBJECTIVE
Protect the Arphann until the Ice Gate is breached.

Set foot to the southern path and accompany the dragon-controlling Arphann to the Ice Gate. Tread the path carefully, as there are hundreds of enemies between you and the gate.

The Arphann arrive at the Ice Gate in strong numbers thanks to your efforts. There they are met by a group of Humans defending the gate.

Rather than 200 defenders, this time the Gate Endurance counter reads 600. Activate an Orb Attack and squash as many Humans as you can. After

filling the Orb Spark meter, let more Humans amass outside the gate before using it.

Help the Arphann and other Outlands tribes push back the Human force while the Arphann dragons swoop down and burn them to a crisp. Meanwhile, dash in and out of the skirmishes, slashing the enemies as you go.

When another group of enemy reinforcements pours in through the Ice Gate, turn on them and slice their numbers down. After a long, arduous battle, Lord Vydenn and Myifee storm onto the field.

Attack Myifee outside the battle lines to make sure it's a fair one-on-one battle. Knock him back so that he's off balance and incapable of counterattacking.

When he attacks, block or dash out of range and return with attacks of your own. Stay on the offensive until Myifee withdraws.

OBJECTIVE
Defeat Lord Vydenn.

Myifee rushes onto the battlefield with Lord Vydenn not far behind. Together they are going to be difficult to defeat. Luckily, the Arphann dragons continue their strafing runs on the Human forces.

Target Myifee first. He is a strong enemy and is capable of cutting through your forces as well.

When Myifee runs off, get to work on Vydenn. He is a powerful warrior, but not impossible to beat. Block his forward dash attack and round behind him to attack his vulnerable spot.

Run your blades through Vydenn until he loses enough health to be scared away. He scurries away like a coward. The Ice Gate has fallen!

CASTLE OF VARRVAZZAR

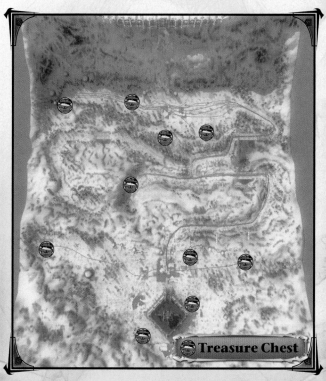

Treasure Chest

Even after they successfully destroyed the Ice Gate, the annihilation of Fort Wyandeek crushed the Goblins. Not only had the Humans taken their brothers, they had also robbed them of their homeland. Dwingvatt and all of the Goblins' hatred are about to collide squarely on Varrvazzar.

The Goblin soldiers pour through the Ice Gate and storm the roads to the Castle of Varrvazzar. The Outlands tribes have united and are marching on the Humans' territory.

Begin the trek to the castle by aiding the Gewgs and Pwucks along the way. Follow the path southeast and join the other tribes momentarily until they are rid of their opposition. If they are stalled along the road, go back and help them eliminate every last Human.

The closer you get to the castle, the stiffer the opposition gets. Luckily, the Orcs have also joined the battle. After you help the Pwucks, Aspharr storms into the fray. Ignore his troops and leave them for the Orcs and other Outlands tribes.

Challenge Aspharr head on and bully him around with your quick strikes. Maneuver him into a corner or against an archer's tower and turn up the heat. Keep him pinned until he retreats like a coward.

Chase Aspharr as he retreats. The Orcs are not far behind, so streak ahead of them and diminish the enemy numbers as you go.

Dodge the boulders by dashing around them when they come careening down at you. Having gotten past the enemies, you reach the castle grounds with the Orcs in tow.

OBJECTIVE
Defeat Varrvazzar's three sons.

The castle is well defended. Varrvazzar's three sons, Vyden, Vyarrhertenn, and Vyertenn have rallied around their cause and protect the south,

east, and west sides of the castle. Together they are very dangerous: one on one, they are manageable.

TIP

Make your fights with the three sons of Varrvazzar easier by eliminating all the enemy archers in the surrounding area.

Trek to the southeast and face Vyertenn on his own grounds. Shove him out of the skirmish lines and pound him with a fury of combo attacks until he falls.

Then, speed over to the west side of the castle and take on Vyden. Take him out, then turn your attention to Vyarrhertenn, who is protecting the south side of the castle. Help Ppakk finish off Vyarrhertenn.

OBJECTIVE
Defeat the castellan, Lord Vydenn.

Proceed to the north of the castle to greet Lord Vydenn. Use an Orb Attack to rid yourself of his bothersome troops, then single him out. Pummel him with strong attacks like Shade and diminish his health bar.

Block or dodge his attacks and sweep around behind him to counterattack. Continue moving around him to keep him guessing, and strike only as he recovers from missed attacks of his own.

After a difficult fight, you wear him down and leave him staggering. Off

balance he is vulnerable. You take a chance and swipe your blade across his chest. It is the final blow. Lord Vydenn is dead and the Castle of Varrvazzar has fallen.

PHOLYA FLATLANDS

Treasure Chest

Although they captured Varrvazzar, the Goblins felt no joy. The report about the slaughter at Fort Wyandeek only fueled hatred toward the Humans. But secretly Dwingvatt felt excitement when he heard that a woman in red armor led the assault on Wyandeek. His vendetta will end here on the Pholya Flatlands.

OBJECTIVE
Destroy the enemy.

King Dwykfarrio has united the Outlands tribes on the Pholya Flatlands. The Goblin king's message of unity rings true to every Outlander. Promising victory, the armies mobilize and begin their final march against the Humans.

Begin your search for the woman in the red armor by rushing across the flatlands. Slash at the Humans on the field as you pass them by, but don't stop to waste time on them. The other Outlanders can handle them.

As you search for the woman, a familiar face resurfaces. Myifee, the mercenary, has returned for a final fight. Give him what he wants.

Meet the mercenary one last time before you re-embark on your vendetta. Stay away from his large sword sweeps and block him when he gets in close.

After dodging an attack, swing around behind him and slice his health bar little by little. Keep your attacks short and sweet, and he will fall.

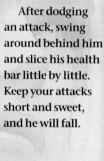

OBJECTIVES
Rescue Dwykfarrio.
Defeat VigkVagk.

After defeating Myifee, put your passionate pursuit on pause. Your king is under attack and desperately needs your help. Though he is perfectly capable of taking out a group of measly Humans, he is also under attack by VigkVagk, a giant Troll.

Dash south and lend him your blades. Ignore the Humans and focus

on the Troll. The Humans help in attacking the Troll, so let them serve as a distraction as you chip away at VigkVagk's health. After he falls, finish off the Humans.

OBJECTIVES
Defeat Inphyy.
Defeat Aspharr.

With Dwykfarrio safe you are free to continue hunting down the woman in red. Just as expected, she runs onto the field. Her brother, Aspharr, is not far behind her. In keeping with the notion of "an eye for an eye," welcome Inphyy to your pain by eliminating her brother first. Shove Aspharr out of range with a few successive powerful combos, then finish him off before she can catch up.

Inphyy will be slightly more difficult to shove around. Single her out by unleashing an Orb Spark on her troops. Once she is the last woman standing, strike her down like you did her brother. Dash around the large sweeping strokes of her sword and pound her from behind.

Her hatred of Goblins is not as powerful as your hatred for her. The battle ends with Inphyy scrambling for her life on the battle-ground.

In a moment of poetic justice, you drive your brother's blade into her back as she drove her blade into his. Your need for vengeance is fulfilled.

Dwykfarrio stands the victor on the Pholya Flatlands. His quest to gain control of the Orb of Light is successful, and his plan for unity among the Outlands tribes is in motion.

He promises to bring stability to the Goblin nation as he brings the Orb of Light and the Orb of Darkness together. A great blinding light engulfs the entire flatlands area...

Age:
12
Class:
Sorceress
Weapon:
Mage's Staff
Orb Spark:
Water

Abandoned as a baby, Tyurru was raised by a great wizard. Although she fights fiercely using Water elements, she still retains the innocence of youth. She carries a large, key-shaped staff.

Raised by old Mylarrvaryss and blessed with great magical talent, she bears an unexpected maturity for her age. Yet deep inside she's just a normal girl. Having grown up in isolation from the outside world, she yearns to visit distant lands.

VITAL STATISTICS

Category	Level 1	Level 2	Level 3	Level 4	Level 5	Level 6	Level 7	Level 8	Level 9
Default Attack Point	100	110	121	133	146	161	177	195	214
Default HP	900	1,350	2,074	2,998	4,200	5,500	8,800	14,266	22,004
Default Defense Point	20	22	24	27	29	32	35	39	43
Default Rate of Critical Hit	12	13	14	15	16	17	18	19	20

COMBO ATTACKS

Tyurru is completely different from any other character. Her attack moves consist of three types—shooting out a stream of water, throwing a mass of water, or creating small waves or geysers. Hydra Shot is very useful to keep the enemies away, and Dagon Wave can be used in close-range combat and boss battles. She is very vulnerable when surrounded by enemies at close range, so pay attention to the enemy's position.

Level 1

Tyurru is the only character with ranged attacks. Because of this, she is vulnerable in close quarters. Make use of her wave attacks to clear out nearby enemies, and Hydra Shot to take down those at a distance.

> **NOTE**
>
> When doing a combo attack, execute button presses separated by commas in quick succession.
> If the move says ", then" or ", press", allow the final move to finish before pressing the next button command.

Move	Execution
Ba'al Rage	Ⓨ,Ⓨ,Ⓨ,Ⓨ,Ⓧ
Dagon Wave	Ⓨ,Ⓨ,Ⓨ,Ⓨ
Even More Waves	Ⓨ,Ⓨ,Ⓨ
Hydra Shot	Ⓧ repeatedly
Jump	Ⓐ
More Waves	Ⓨ, Ⓨ
Puffier Liva-tan	Jump, then press Ⓨ
Puffy Liva-tan	ⓁⓉ+Ⓧ
Remora Shot	Jump, then press Ⓧ repeatedly
Treat	Ⓧ repeatedly, then press Ⓨ
Water Geysers	During Orb Attack, press Ⓧ
Water Splash	During Orb Attack, press Ⓨ
Wave	Ⓨ

Level 2

Level 2 introduces Tyurru's most useful move, Scylla Trip. With it you can travel longer distances safely and escape from harm.

Move	Execution
Heavy!	Move while pushing a mass of water
Outta Here!	ⓁⓉ+Ⓨ
Scylla Trip	Jump, then press Ⓐ repeatedly

Level 3

Needle Nereid is a great addition to your arsenal at level 3. Use it to attack enemies in high places or to rain down death from above.

Move	Execution
Needle Nereid	Jump, press Ⓐ repeatedly, then press Ⓧ
Take That!	While pushing a mass of water, press Ⓧ
Triton Smash	Press Ⓧ repeatedly, then hold Ⓨ

Level 4

Much like level 1's Even More Waves, Water Wave is a great attack to clear out enemies at close range.

Move	Execution
Siren Wave	While pushing a mass of water, press Ⓨ
Water Wave	Ⓨ,Ⓨ,Ⓨ,Ⓧ

Level 5

Lizardman and Ba'al is a great defensive move that pushes enemies away. Just remember to follow up with a debilitating attack.

Move	Execution
Kraken Bash	While pushing a large mass of water, press Ⓨ
Liva-tan Burst	Burst a large mass of water by pressing Ⓧ
Lizardman and Ba'al	ⓁⓉ, then hold Ⓨ
Really Heavy!	Move while pushing a large mass of water
Take THAT!	While pushing a large mass of water, press Ⓧ

Level 6

Level 6's Lorelei Shower is a great attack to complement Scylla Trip and Needle Nereid. With it, you drop water bombs on enemies.

Move	Execution
Lorelei Shower	Jump, press Ⓐ repeatedly, then press Ⓨ

Level 7

Another in a long line of wave attacks, this one drains your Orb Attack gauge. Make sure it is worth it before using it.

Move	Execution
Another Water Wave	Ⓨ,Ⓨ,Ⓨ, then hold Ⓧ (drains Orb Attack gauge)

Level 8

It's not much different from Another Water Wave, but Water Wave Special is significantly more powerful.

Move	Execution
Water Wave Special	Ⓨ,Ⓨ,Ⓨ, then hold Ⓧ (drains Orb Attack gauge)

Level 9

This is the last of Tyurru's wave attacks. Replacing the previous two attacks, Water Wave Gorgeous ups the ante in terms of destructive power.

Move	Execution
Water Wave Gorgeous	ⓨ, ⓨ, ⓨ, then hold ⓧ (drains Orb Attack gauge)

WEAPONS

Tyurru's staves are interesting weapons. Shaped like large keys, they unlock the hidden potential in Tyurru. Because she doesn't actually strike at her enemies with her staves, they serve more as focusing agents than as weapons.

School Staff

Level 1

A magic student's training staff, this is Tyurru's default weapon.

Wizard Wand

Level 1

This powerful staff is granted to wizards; it raises Attack power by 10 percent and critical rate by 20.

Antique Rod

Level 2

A staff that emits a dazzling light, this rod increases Orb appear rate by 20 percent, critical rate by 40 percent, and Speed by 10 percent.

Mana Wand

Level 3

This wand boosts the concentration of its wielder. Allies' Attack power amplifies 20 percent, Speed increases by 10 percent, Orb Attack length rises by 30 percent, and the Orb appear rate goes up 30 percent when Mana Wand is equipped.

Rainbow Wand

Level 3

The Rainbow Wand was brought to earth by a spirit. When it is equipped, Attack power goes up 60 percent, Orb appear rate increases by 20 percent, and Speed goes up 20 percent. As an added bonus, it revives fallen allies.

Prime Key

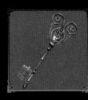

Level 4

A golden key staff that wields immense power, this weapon augments Attack power and Orb gauge charge rate by 20 percent, while critical rate goes up 40 percent. Orb appear rate increases by 10 percent.

Memory Mace

Level 6

A memento from Mylarrvaryss, this weapon enhances Attack power and critical rate by 50 percent. Speed goes up 20 percent, and Item drop rate rises 60 percent.

Weapon Locations and Conditions

Weapon	Location/Condition
School Staff	Default weapon
Wizard Wand	Treasure chest past the North Gate of Varrgandd
Antique Rod	Clear Varrgandd Mission with A Rank
Mana Wand	Northeast corner of Eaurvarria map
Prime Key	Treasure chest in Fort Wyandeek Mission
Memory Mace	Clear Pholya Flatlands mission with A Rank
Rainbow Wand	Clear Eaurvarria Mountains mission with over 2,000 kill count

A MAGICAL JOURNEY

Tyurru is a young sorceress, indeed. But when her mentor Mylarrvaryss warns her of the impending war, she is quick to take sides.

Before charging out to battle, however, she must find her element. She passes one final challenge from Mylarrvaryss and sets off to an elemental cave. There she unlocks Liva-tan, her elemental spirit of Water. With Liva-tan floating behind her, she sets off to the war between Humans and Goblins.

BASTIDE OF VARRGANDD

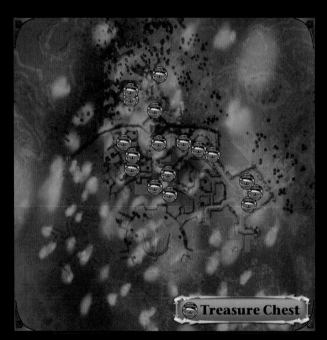

🛡 **Treasure Chest**

After leaving the side of great wizard Mylarrvaryss, Tyurru is bestowed with the protection of the Light and the power of Water elements. This is her first time on the battlefield. Intense fighting has erupted both inside and outside the Bastide of Varrgandd.

OBJECTIVE
Destroy the enemies outside Varrgandd castle.

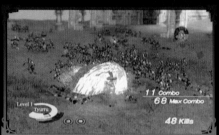

The area outside of Varrgandd castle is infested with Goblins. You must help the people of the Bastide of Varrgandd or it will fall! Spray the enemies with your water attacks and clean the area outside the castle.

CAUTION

Do not allow yourself to be surrounded by Goblins; your defense is vulnerable to close-quarters combat and you will be unable to recover.

OBJECTIVE
Defeat the Troll.

Trolls, just great. They must be strengthening their defenses.

Stay near Myifee on the battlegrounds to ensure you have backup should you find yourself in a rut. Sure enough, before long the Goblins strengthen their defenses with a Troll.

Take on the Troll and eliminate him. Use strong combos like Even More Waves and only use Hydra Shot when you have a clear shot at his back. Knock the Troll back with geyser attacks and pepper him with Hydra Shots as he runs away. Stay on the creature until he dies.

OBJECTIVE
Destroy the enemy at the North and East Gates.

Once the gate opens up, rush in to confront the enemies inside. The North Gate is still on verge of being overrun, so back up Myifee and wash away all the encroaching Goblins.

After the North Gate is washed clean of Goblin gunk, gather the troops with ⓇⒷ and ⓁⒷ and lead them southeast, toward the East Gate.

Traverse the market streets with Myifee until you run into Yesperratt as she battles a few Goblins of her own. Help her out so that she is free to join your motley crew.

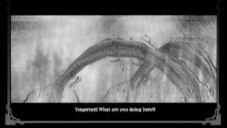

Yesperratt! What are you doing here?!

Lead the group, Myifee and Yesperratt included, to the East Gate. There, the castle defenders are having a rough time driving back the assaulting hordes. Spray down the Goblin filth and fill up your Orb Attack gauge and your Orb Spark meter.

Stay near Yesperratt and Myifee for a strong defense. Clear out the Goblin troops at the East Gate and wait to use your Orb attacks. More of their reinforcements are on the way.

When the new wave of Goblin attackers attempts to invade the castle, back away from the main gate and run back to the market entrance where you came from.

Turn around and unleash your Orb Spark attack. As the tsunami finishes washing away the invaders in the gate entrance, storm ahead and help Yesperratt finish off the second wave that attacks.

VigkVagk's support troops are so numerous that your Orb Spark meter fills right away. Once again, back away and take aim at the remaining troops—let your Orb Spark tsunami free.

When all is said and done, VigkVagk is the only enemy standing. Take turns attacking VigkVagk with Yesperratt. When she draws his attention, attack him from behind. When you draw his attention, run and lead him toward Yesperratt so she can attack.

**OBJECTIVE
Defeat VigkVagk.**

With the second wave of enemies defeated, the Goblins send in VigkVagk in a last-ditch effort to crumble you. Gather more red Orbs to fill your Orb Attack gauge and release it as soon as it is ready.

Continue this strategic game of cat and mouse to slowly erode VigkVagk's health. After a few rounds about the gate's plaza, the Troll falls and is no more.

Impressed with your ability to fight, Myifee, Badokk, and Epharr invite you to face the Goblins at Fort Wyandeek while they go to rescue the Castle of Varrvazzar.

Always eager to please, you jump at the chance to help out once again. You may be a small-scale sorceress, but this is a full-scale war.

EAURVARRIA MOUNTAINS

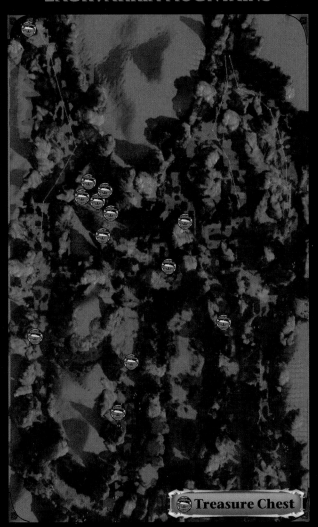

After lending her strength at Varrgandd and becoming a soldier in the Army of Light, Tyurru heads for the Goblin stronghold at Fort Wyandeek. Along the way she encounters Goblin forces in the Eaurvarria Mountains but is ecstatic at another chance to test her skills.

OBJECTIVE
Reach the rally point.

The path across the Eaurvarria Mountains is extremely dangerous. Spiked booby traps, boulders, and high perches with archers, all block the way between you and the rally point.

The best way to traverse this area is to do it quickly. Drown the attacking Goblins and fill your Orb Attack gauge right away. Once it is full, save it to be used deeper in the mountains.

Use Scylla Trip to glide over spiked booby traps with ease; stop only to land and relaunch yourself into the air. When flying over enemies, press ✗ repeatedly to rain attacks on them.

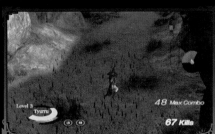

CAUTION

Just because the spikes on the floor aren't visible doesn't mean they aren't there. Watch your step!

Treasure Chest

Proceed north until you reach the first of many forks in the road. There you encounter a sizable Goblin force. Wash them away before proceeding.

At the first fork, choose the left path. Your destination is the far northwest corner of the map, so don't dillydally!

After setting on the leftmost path, blast away the enemies perched atop the fallen tree trunks. Leap into the air with Scylla Trip and torpedo them with water.

Upon landing, unleash your Orb Attack on the Goblin army that has amassed at the next intersection just to the left of the fallen tree trunk.

Take the adjacent path leading west and follow it as it wends north. There you encounter a Goblin captain and his goons. Target the Goblin wizards first or they will make life miserable by interrupting your spells and slowing you down.

Then, pound the other troops with Ba'al Rage and hold back the Goblin captain. When he tries to attack, attack him with Puffy Liva-tan. Wear him down until he is out of your way.

Continue north, using Scylla Trip to avoid spikes and Remora Shot to eliminate enemies up on high. Slay enough enemies to fill your Orb Attack gauge. You will need it very soon. Turn left again and follow the path as it makes a sharp turn southwest.

When you reach the first adjacent pathway leading west, take it. It is a valuable shortcut that will save you much heartache.

After taking the shortcut west, follow the path as it turns north toward the rally point. Spring into the air and fly hurriedly across the sky, avoiding enemies by leaving them behind. The enemies will follow you north to the rally point, but that is OK. Let them form a long stream of foes on

the mountainside floors.

Fly ahead of them and land just before you reach the rally point. Leap over or sprint around the incoming boulders, then turn on your river of enemies and unleash an Orb Attack. The resulting blue Orbs should fill your Orb Spark nearly right away. When it's full, open the floodgates and let your Orb Spark wash the mountainsides.

This leaves only the Troll standing. With you and he alone at the rally point, the fight will be one of endurance.

Goad the Troll to attack by standing directly in front of him, then as he approaches, fly past him and land right away. Upon landing, immediately turn around and blast

him from behind. Repeat this until the Troll is drenched and drowned. With the path behind you washed clean, leave the mountainous area and continue toward Fort Wyandeek.

NOTE

The Troll is fast. He will occasionally spin around and catch you when you land. If he does, use Outta Here or Puffy Liva-tan to cause more damage!

BRANCHING PATH TALE

The mountain pathways can be a little confusing. In the labyrinthine web of twists and turns, it is easy to get lost. If you do, use the following directions to find your way to the rally point:

1. From the starting point head north.
2. At the first fork in the road, take the left path.
3. Take the first left. It leads west.
4. Immediately turn right and follow the path north.
5. Make a sharp turn left as the path leads west, then south.
6. Follow the path south.
7. Take the very first turn right.
8. Make one more right and follow the path north.

FORT WYANDEEK

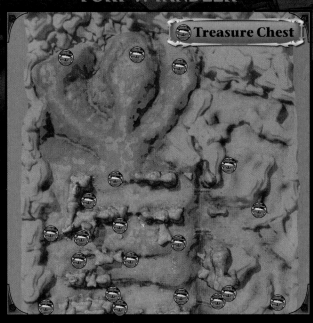

Treasure Chest

The Temple Knights have already breached the fortress, and the battle is underway. Tyurru, anxious and excited for Inphyy and Aspharr to see her progress, has yet to learn the true horror of sorrow and war.

OBJECTIVE
Defeat the Goblin corporals.

TIP

Before rushing off to war, remember to activate the troops behind you for support!

You finally made it to Fort Wyandeek, where Inphyy and Aspharr can be witness to your powers. But before they can see what you can do, you have to find them.

Rush out and follow the path as it leads you east, toward the Goblin corporals. Battle the Goblin hordes along the way and keep your feet on the ground. Flying over

the enemy will only draw them into a large, unmanageable bunch.

Reach the enemy corporals safely, just in time to see the wooden bridge crumble and give way. The corporals don't take kindly to your presence and immediately attack you. Return the warm greeting and blast them with your magic.

Drop their troops and concentrate fire on them. They

can push through your waterspouts, so be careful. Back off, gain a safe distance, then reassume your attack until the corporals fall.

OBJECTIVE
Join the Temple Knights.

The gates open up when the corporals fall. Turn back and run east until you reach the gate. Defeat the enemies guarding it and pass through, penetrating north, deeper into the fort.

The enemies turn up the heat inside the fort and come storming down on you. Leap into the air and do a strafing run right over them. Blast them to cool them off.

Round the corner and keep heading north. Eventually the path turns east, toward the rally point at the center of the Fort Wyandeek.

Around the corner is another large group of Goblins. As they are just about to crash down around you, use an Orb Spark attack to drown them in a flood.

OBJECTIVE
Defeat the Goblin wizards.

Now that you've just washed away a troop of Goblins, the Goblin wizard is left without guards to help protect him. This makes him a wide-open target for your waterworks.

Stay on the move to avoid his black magic spells, and pelt him with watery attacks. Splash the wizard repeatedly, until he is all washed up.

Follow Inphyy and Aspharr into the Goblin stronghold. Their troops prepare to face off against the Goblins guarding the altar. Meanwhile, attack the Goblin wizard to the right of the altar.

Destroy the wizard before he can lay waste to your troops and cause major damage to your war efforts. Afterward, run back toward the altar and dash up the western hill that leads to the Goblin huts.

After picking yourself up, dash back down the hill toward the central area of the fort. Finish off straggling Goblin soldiers as you go to fill your Orb Spark gauge.

At the base of the hill, turn left and scurry up the middle pathway toward the altar. Three more wizards await! Upon reaching the top of the hill, release your Orb Spark and clean the altar of Goblins with your tidal waves.

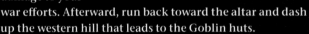

A second wizard is hiding behind the village huts. Hunt him down and dispatch him as you did his counterpart.

The Orb Spark clears the area of all other Goblins, but the three wizards don't drown. They take major damage, leaving them vulnerable to your standard attacks. Leap into the air and finish them off with Remora Shot or Needle Nereid.

The wizard lies slain on the village ground. But he lies amidst a sea of Goblin bodies, not all soldiers. The attack on Fort Wyandeek was not only a strategic strike to help win the war, it was also Inphyy's personal massacre of innocent Goblin women and children.

You fall to your knees, buckled by the devastation, but Klarrann assures you that though these are atrocities of war, *your* efforts must continue. Others may pursue their own causes, but your intentions are still pure and good.

Shocked by his sister's actions, Aspharr confronts Inphyy. "What have you done?" he asks. But the red knight stands behind her orders to kill every last Goblin in the fort, no matter if they were younglings.

Yesperratt's actions were just as shocking to you. Though she claims she was only following Inphyy's orders, it was Yesperratt's magic that murdered the Wyandeek Goblins. Before you can press the issue with Yesperratt, word comes of the Goblins' march on the Pholya Flatlands. Though you don't want to fight anymore, this war must end now before more innocents die.

PHOLYA FLATLANDS

 **Treasure Chest**

The horrible incident at Fort Wyandeek has filled Tyurru with a deep, unspeakable unease. As forces of Light and Dark clash on the Pholya Flatlands, screams like she's never heard before fill her ears. And with this, Tyurru begins to think deeply about the true meaning of war.

Standing atop the hill on the Pholya Flatlands, you witness the brutal nature of war. Goblins and Humans crash into each other as carnage breaks out on an otherwise beautiful landscape.

As the horror overcomes you, Liva-tan reminds you that you must do something. You agree and leap into action.

OBJECTIVE
Join the Temple Knights and destroy the enemy.

Scamper down the hill and attack the Goblin soldiers as they battle with the Human army. Two small skirmishes rage on at the base of the hill.

Alternate between both skirmishes to aid both troops equally. Ignore Aspharr and Inphyy's squabble; your priority is to ensure that as many of your troops survive as possible.

While these two skirmishes die down, Gewg reinforcements approach from the east. Collect your support troops and leave these battles behind. Go wash and squash the Gewgs!

The Gewg force is of medium size, yet perfectly compacted into ranks. Streak over their ranks, blasting them with Needle Nereid as you pass. Land on the other side of the army and turn around to do a return run. Meanwhile, your forces clash with the remaining Gewgs.

CAUTION

The Gewg forces break rank almost immediately—don't let yourself be surrounded!

OBJECTIVE
Defeat Dwingvatt.

The Gewgs wash out of the battle, but a new problem has arisen. Dwingvatt, the white Goblin, streaks onto the field ready for a fight. He is on a mission of vengeance, searching for his brother's murderer. However, anyone that stands in his way is fair game.

Lucky for you, his fight is with Inphyy. Back off as he brings the fight to Inphyy and support her troops instead. Bust down Dwingvatt's troops with your water, and let the white Goblin's health dwindle as he faces off against Inphyy and Aspharr.

When Dwingvatt's troops are low enough in numbers for your guards to manage, turn the waterworks on Dwingvatt and help the knightly siblings destroy the hate-filled Goblin.

Blast him with wave attacks from behind, and back off when Inphyy delivers blows of her own. After suffering Aspharr's pounding, Inphyy's slashes, Yesperratt's earth-shattering combos, and your watery attacks, Dwingvatt dies on the Pholya Flatlands.

OBJECTIVE
Find Dwykfarrio and defeat him.

Having bested Dwykfarrio's best soldier, begin your hunt for the Goblin king. Explore the northeast corner of the map and you will find the cowardly king hidden in the misty hillock.

As soon as you find Dwykfarrio, eliminate his complement of troops. Wash them away with an Orb Spark and leave the Goblin king exposed. Aspharr and Inphyy arrive on the scene and immediately begin their attack.

Help the powerful threesome of Aspharr, Inphyy, and Yesperratt keep the Goblin leader on the ground. As Yesperratt knocks him down with an earthquake blast, follow up with an elemental attack of your own.

When Inphyy and Aspharr are not attacking him, blast him with Hydra Shot to keep him on the defensive and allow the siblings to rush him from behind as he blocks your blows. The constant barrage of attacks from the four of you proves to be too much for Dwykfarrio to handle, and he perishes.

With Dwyk-farrio defeated, you, Mylarrvaryss, and Yesperratt convene on the flatlands. Mylar-rvaryss enlightens you about the division between the Light and Dark Orbs. He tells you how they should not be brought together, and "those that touch the Light should not touch the Dark and those that touch the Dark should not touch the Light."

Incapable of grasping the notion that the Dark Orb is far too powerful to control, Yesperratt argues that the sorcerers, with all their power, should be able to take possession of the Dark Orb. Temporarily dissuaded by Mylarrvaryss, Yesperratt joins you in squashing the Arphann reinforcements.

OBJECTIVE
Destroy the Arphann.

The Arphann are not too far ahead. Head southwest and meet them along the hill's base. There, blast them with your water geysers and absorb their Orbs. If you are nearly finished filling the Orb Attack gauge and/or the Orb Spark meter, top them off now.

OBJECTIVE
Find Yesperratt.

Continue moving south until you find Yesperratt engaged in battle with Mylarrvaryss. Convinced that she can control the Dark Orb, she is seduced by its power and mortally wounds Mylarrvaryss. Yesperratt is an extremely powerful sorceress capable of killing you with one attack, so be quick.

Before she turns her murderous intentions on you, leave her vicinity and go get help. Explore the southern countryside across the bridge while Yesperratt calmly follows behind you. When you encounter a group of Goblins, get near them and draw them toward you, leading them to Yesperratt.

NOTE

As the saying goes, "an enemy of my enemy is a friend of mine."

Remember that while Yesperratt has turned on you, she has not aligned herself with the Goblins. They are still an enemy to both of you and they don't hesitate to engage the traitorous sorceress.

TIP

Another group of Goblins is camped at the western edge of the flatlands. Recruit them as well if Yesperratt is too much to handle on your own.

As soon as the Goblins engage Yesperratt, distance yourself from the fight. Allow the two forces to collide and whittle away at each other.

Though Yesperratt is powerful, she has to contend with enemy wizards as well. Holding them off is a difficult task when her attacks

are interrupted by Goblin grunts. As they fight, frequently sweep over the battle and attack with Needle Nereid and Lorelei Shower. Pause outside the battle lines, sneak up behind Yesperratt, and blast her with Puffier Liva-tan until she breaks.

CAUTION

One of Yesperratt's attacks, where she sends multiple streams of earth at you, is very dangerous and capable of killing you almost instantly.

With Yesperratt slain and Mylar-rvaryss on the brink of death, you kneel by your mentor's side to hear his last words.

He entrusts you to take control in his place and continue the spirit of the grand wizard. Hesitant at first, you say no. But realizing that you have matured, and with Liva-tan by your side, you decide to honor his wish.

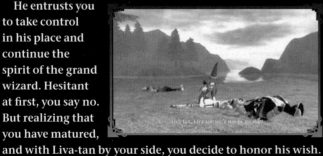

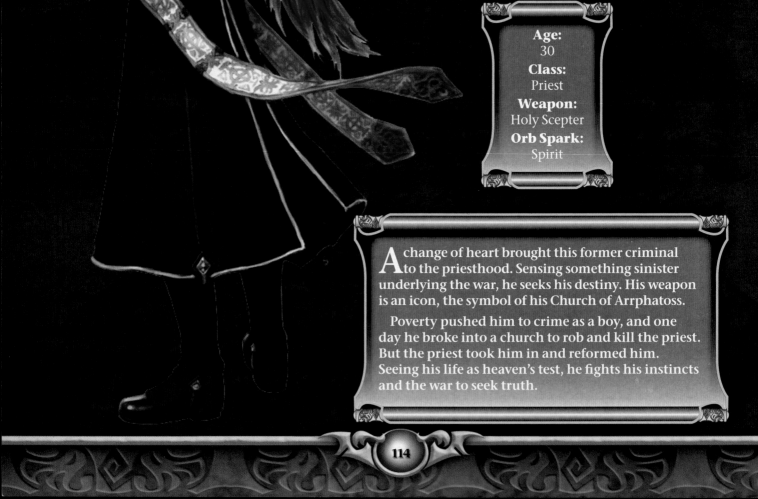

Age:
30
Class:
Priest
Weapon:
Holy Scepter
Orb Spark:
Spirit

A change of heart brought this former criminal to the priesthood. Sensing something sinister underlying the war, he seeks his destiny. His weapon is an icon, the symbol of his Church of Arrphatoss.

Poverty pushed him to crime as a boy, and one day he broke into a church to rob and kill the priest. But the priest took him in and reformed him. Seeing his life as heaven's test, he fights his instincts and the war to seek truth.

VITAL STATISTICS

Category	Level 1	Level 2	Level 3	Level 4	Level 5	Level 6	Level 7	Level 8	Level 9
Default Attack Point	100	110	121	133	146	161	177	195	214
Default HP	1,100	1,460	1,926	2,726	4,220	5,500	8,800	14,266	23,224
Default Defense Point	20	22	24	27	29	32	35	39	43
Default Rate of Critical Hit	12	13	14	15	16	17	18	19	20

COMBO ATTACKS

Klarrann does not rely on long chain combos. His moves are slower than those of other characters', but each of his attacks is very powerful. Almost all of his moves can disable an enemy's guard. Kneel Before Spirits, for example, has a high chance of disabling enemies' defenses and stunning them at the same time. Mix up the throwing attacks that begin with Thou Art Forgiven and the weapon-transforming attacks to defeat enemies quickly.

Level 1

Klarrann's level 1 attacks are short, powerful bursts of divine strength. Capable of channeling holy energy through his scepter, Klarrann is a danger to all who oppose him.

NOTE

When doing a combo attack, execute button presses separated by commas in quick succession.

If the move says ", then" or ", press", allow the final move to finish before pressing the next button command.

Move	Execution
Be as Dust	Ⓧ,Ⓧ,Ⓧ,Ⓧ
Die Without Straying	Ⓧ,Ⓧ,Ⓧ,Ⓧ, then press Ⓨ
Fall from Grace	During Ⓧ,Ⓧ,Ⓨ, press Ⓡ+Ⓧ or Ⓡ+Ⓨ
Flee	Ⓡ
Have No Thirst	Ⓨ,Ⓨ,Ⓨ
Judgment	During Orb Attack, press Ⓨ
Kneel Before Spirits	Ⓐ
Moan	Ⓨ,Ⓧ, then hold Ⓧ
Perish Together	During Ⓧ,Ⓧ,Ⓨ, walk
Pray!	During Ⓧ,Ⓧ,Ⓨ, press Ⓧ
Punishment	Ⓡ, then press Ⓧ or Ⓨ
Repent	Ⓧ,Ⓨ
Salvation	During Ⓧ,Ⓧ,Ⓨ, press Ⓧ,Ⓧ
Sin's Burden	During Ⓧ,Ⓧ,Ⓨ, press Ⓡ
Take This Sword	During Orb Attack, press Ⓧ
Thou Shalt Perish	Ⓧ,Ⓧ,Ⓨ

Level 2

Level 2 introduces a series of invaluable moves that begin with To Thy Rest. Learn this move well; you will rely on it heavily.

Move	Execution
Bequeath Unto Thee	During Ⓧ,Ⓧ,Ⓨ, press Ⓨ,Ⓨ
Despair	Ⓨ,Ⓧ, then press Ⓡ
Shout	Ⓨ,Ⓧ, then press Ⓧ,Ⓧ
Thou Art Forgiven	Ⓧ,Ⓨ,Ⓨ
To Thy Journey	During Ⓧ,Ⓧ,Ⓧ,Ⓨ, walk
To Thy Rest	Ⓧ,Ⓧ,Ⓧ,Ⓨ
Trial from Spirits	During Ⓧ,Ⓧ,Ⓧ,Ⓨ, then press Ⓧ
You Worthless...!	Ⓨ,Ⓧ (drains Orb Attack gauge)

Level 3

Have No Hunger is a strong combination that is best used after stunning an opponent. However, the true gem of Klarrann's level 3 moves is Return to the Soil. With it, he can clear enemies as they crowd around him in close quarters.

Move	Execution
Fall to Hell	Ⓧ,Ⓧ,Ⓧ,Ⓨ, then press Ⓨ
Have No Hunger	Ⓨ,Ⓨ,Ⓨ,Ⓨ
Quake with Fear	Ⓨ,Ⓨ,Ⓧ, then press Ⓡ
Return to the Soil	Ⓧ repeatedly, then press Ⓧ
Struggle	Ⓨ,Ⓨ,Ⓧ, then press Ⓧ,Ⓧ
Writhe in Agony	Ⓨ,Ⓨ,Ⓧ, then hold Ⓧ
You Wish to Die?!	Ⓨ,Ⓨ,Ⓧ (drains Orb Attack gauge)

Level 4

At level 4 Klarrann learns two moves that drain his Orb Attack gauge. Don't Anger Me and Repent Before Spirits both prove very useful in felling strong opponents.

Move	Execution
Don't Anger Me	Ⓨ,Ⓨ,Ⓨ,Ⓧ (drains Orb Attack gauge)
Die That Way	Ⓨ,Ⓨ,Ⓨ,Ⓧ, then press Ⓡ
Flick	Ⓡ, then press Ⓨ
No Escape	Ⓨ,Ⓨ,Ⓨ,Ⓧ, then hold Ⓧ
No Mercy	Ⓨ,Ⓨ,Ⓨ,Ⓧ, then press Ⓧ,Ⓧ
Repent Before Spirits	Ⓧ,Ⓧ,Ⓧ,Ⓧ,Ⓧ,Ⓨ (drains Orb Attack gauge)

Level 5

Level 5 introduces a new finishing move to Klarrann's To Thy Rest combo attack.

Move	Execution
Sublimation	During Ⓧ,Ⓧ,Ⓧ,Ⓨ, press Ⓨ,Ⓧ (drains Orb Attack gauge)

Level 6

Short and sweet, Disappear drains your Orb Attack gauge, so don't rely on it too heavily.

Move	Execution
Disappear!	⊗,⊗,⊙, then hold ⊗ (drains Orb Attack gauge)

HOLY SCEPTERS

Klarrann has no need for fancy swords or gimmicky weapons. He is more concerned with preventing the King of Nights from succeeding than he is about having a fancy weapon. That is why large blunt objects are perfectly fine for his needs.

Antique Icon

Level 1

This religious icon was enshrined at the church in Varrgandd. It is Klarrann's starting weapon.

Roar

Level 2

Roar purifies evil thoughts and objects. It increases Attack power and Attack range by 10 percent.

Punishment

Level 3

A cane that eliminates an opponent without inflicting pain, this weapon boosts Attack power, Defense power, and Attack range by 20 percent.

Sentence

Level 3

Sentence is a rod of transmigration and a legendary item of the heavens. With it, Klarrann's Attack range rises 50 percent; his Orb Attack gauge and Orb Spark gauge increase at the same rate.

Sentinel

Level 4

A mace of punishment that brings out remorse, Sentinel boosts Attack power and Attack range by 30 percent, and critical rate by 20.

Staff of Slumber

Level 5

This is a mace of eternal rest that releases the body and brings peace. Attack range goes up 40 percent and critical rate is 100 percent when this is equipped.

Cane of Faith

Level 5

A miraculous cane that gathers power from strong belief, the Cane of Faith boosts Attack range 40 percent, Defense power 50 percent, and Guard break rate 50 percent.

Weapon Locations and Conditions

Weapon	Location/Condition
Antique Icon	Default weapon
Roar	Kill the first Troll Klarann encounters
Punishment	Clear the Varrgandd Mission with A Rank
Sentence	Dropped when all Varrgandd citizens are rescued
Sentinel	Treasure chest in Fort Wyandeek Mission
Staff of Slumber	Kill all of Ninety-Nine Night's Army in Pholya Mission
Cane of Faith	Treasure chest in Pholya Mission

HOLY MAN, HOLY WAR

As a priest at the Church of Arrphatoss, Klarrann's days are often busy. One day, as he goes about his business in the church, a messenger storms in screaming about impending war between the Humans and the Goblins.

Recognizing that the time has come for him to pick up his holy scepter, Klarrann springs into action.

BASTIDE OF VARRGANDD

Treasure Chest

Klarrann notices that the Goblins are preparing for a battle larger than he has ever seen before. But why would the Goblins be looking to start such a large-scale battle now? Klarrann can't shake the feeling in his gut. He knows something horrible is about to happen.

OBJECTIVES
Defeat the Goblins and rescue their Human captives.
Lead the captives to the West Gate.

What should have been a normal day at the church became the first day of a long and trying journey. The Bastide of Varrgandd is under siege, and Humans are being taken captive by Goblins.

They've made it this far. We must protect the civilians first.

Run southwest and smite your enemies as you go. At the southwest corner of the plaza is a group

of Humans under attack by misguided Goblins. Strike down the Goblins with your scepter and round up the frightened Humans.

Lead the Humans through the market streets to the West Gate. Along the way you encounter small groups of Goblins. They are easy to dispatch but must be eliminated quickly.

Because they are after the civilians, the Goblins ignore you at first and attack them instead. Intercept the Goblin

attackers before they reach the Humans and kill them. Use Kneel Before Spirits to stun them first, then strike them down with more powerful attacks.

TIP

Smash the surrounding chests to get Healing Wood and stay near your followers to keep them constantly healed.

Near the West Gate, Goblins and a Troll stand ready. Slowly approach them and goad them into attacking you in the narrow market streets. When they do, use an Orb Attack to cut them down.

Like the giant tree that he is, chop down the enemy Troll. If he is left for last, he can swipe at the Humans you escort and end the mission prematurely. Get the villagers past the Troll and they are able to escape through the West Gate.

You've rescued the villagers and escorted them to the West Gate, but the Goblin threat is not vanquished yet. A white Goblin penetrates the castle defenses and poses a threat. These Goblins are very rare, so there must be something very special about this Goblin.

A white Goblin? Are they still being born even in this age?

Rush down the castle streets killing Goblins as you go. Keep your nose pointed south on your way to face the white Goblin at the main gate.

The white Goblin is unbelievably fast, so don't try to keep up with him. Speed is not your forte—power is. Use Kneel Before Spirits to stun the

Goblin when he rushes you, then follow up with strong two-to three-hit combos like Have No Thirst. Keep your guard up when he attacks in close quarters, and follow up with the stun and strike combos until he falls.

The white Goblin was proof enough that there is something different about this war. Perhaps the pale-skinned beast is an omen. Regardless, the battle has just begun and you are needed at Fort Wyandeek.

FORT WYANDEEK

Treasure Chest

They are past the point of no return; war is now inevitable. But Klarrann, believing that his true duty is to put an end to this futile conflict, is hunting for answers. He knows the key to the truth lies within Fort Wyandeek, and he makes his way to the battlefield.

NOTE

Because Klarrann is not a captain, he does not have a buffet of troops to choose from before setting off to the battle.

Before eagerly setting out for Fort Wyandeek, take a second to look around. Two squads of infantry wait behind you, ready for action. Use ⓇⒷ and ⓁⒷ to activate them and lead them into battle.

OBJECTIVE
Defeat the guard.

Rush out of the gates and into Fort Wyandeek. Goblin archers and grunts are stationed just beyond your starting point.

As you enter the fort, make a sharp right and swing around, running uphill to face the Goblin guard. Crush him and his goons to open up the first gate.

OBJECTIVE
Destroy all the enemies in the plaza.

Rush past the gate and immediately turn left. Leave your troops behind the gate so they are not bowled over by the boulders rolling down the plaza hill.

Once the boulders are no longer an issue, regroup the infantry and storm up the hill to face Ppakk the Third. If you have enough to release an Orb Attack, use it on his Pwucks. Then, just as you felled the white Goblin, stun the Pwuck king before attacking with short chain combos.

Transform your weapon into a giant holy hammer by pressing Y and immediately holding X. With the giant hammer in your hands,

smite the Pwuck king and keep him down. Once he is defeated, the gate behind you opens.

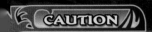
CAUTION

Don't use the weapon transformation moves too often; they drain you Orb Attack gauge, leaving you high and dry when you need it.

OBJECTIVES
Join Inphyy and Aspharr.
Destroy the Orcs.

Cross the southern gate that opened at Ppakk's defeat and follow the road west. Cross the wooden bridge and dash across the valley to rendezvous with Inphyy and Aspharr.

The siblings are locked in battle with five Orc battalions. Lend them your help until all five battalions are defeated and an angry Troll shows up.

Rush at the Troll and strike him with your scepter. Block his thunderous attacks and counterattack with your own. Your strength is almost on par with his, which makes for an inte esting battle of behemoths.

Keep swatting him back until he no longer gets up. The next gate opens and the brother-sister duo rushes in ahead of you.

OBJECTIVE
Defeat the Trolls by the altar.

Follow Inphyy and Aspharr deeper into the fort. Just outside the Goblin altar they clash weapons with more Goblins and their troll companions.

Help Aspharr and Inphyy while filling your Orb Attack gauge. If you are nearly finished filling your Orb Spark meter, top it off now.

With the fort clean of enemy resistance, you are able to read the markings on the Goblin altar. They tell of a meeting between the 99 Nights king and the Goblin king, Dwykfarrio.

This is worse than you thought....

Save your Orb Spark for now and finish off Inphyy and Aspharr's enemies. If possible, try to fill up your Orb Attack gauge as well. Both will come in handy.

After topping off your gauges, turn your attention to the hill leading up to the altar. Calmly approach the altar and annihilate the enemies at the altar with your Orb Spark attack. This leaves only the two Trolls to contend with.

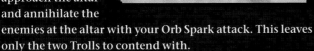

PHOLYA FLATLANDS

Treasure Chest

Collect all the power-ups left behind by the Goblin presence atop the hill and approach the two Trolls. Wait until they are near each other, then activate your Orb Attack.

Swat at them with your powered-up scepter until their health bars are nearly empty. Finish the Trolls

off with your holy hammer attack. When the Trolls fall, so does Fort Wyandeek.

Klarrann's worst fear has come true. Dwykfarrio knows the secret of the Orb, and the legendary King of Nights is trying to control events through Dwykfarrio. Something will happen at the final showdown on the Pholya Flatlands, and Klarrann is prepared to risk his life to stop the King of Nights' evil plans.

The sun is growing dark over the Pholya Flatlands. Surely this is another omen that the coming of the 99 Nights is at hand.

You meet with Syumerrt on the battlefield before the fighting erupts to discuss what is on the verge of happening. Decided on stopping the King of Nights' events from unfolding, you go your separate ways.

Since the day the Orb was divided into Light and Darkness, there has been strife. The two separate orbs call out to another, always compelled in folklore if those orbs were to become one again, even we don't know what would happen. Isn't it that it would not be good.

The fog hides the approaching armies. From the west march the armies of Humans; from the east approach the Goblin hordes. You are trapped in the middle.

Rush east at the Goblin front lines and punish them with your scepter. Fill your Orb Attack gauge and save it for a later time.

OBJECTIVE
Destroy the enemy.

The Army of Darkness converges around you just as the battle begins. Clearly, it is the King of Nights that is behind this war. Dwykfarrio is only a puppet in all of this.

This is no time to ponder things, however; now you must destroy the Army of Darkness.

OBJECTIVE
Defeat Dwingvatt.

Suddenly, the white Goblin, Dwingvatt, returns with a Goblin force. They are not the only ones, however. More troops of the King of Nights' Army of Darkness float onto the field.

Leave the Human warriors behind to face the Outlanders while you sprint southeast to meet Dwingvatt head on.

Strike at Dwingvatt to engage him, then let him follow you out of the fog. Draw him out of the foggy hilltop and to the base of the hill below, where you can better see your opponent.

Once there, engage him again and strike him down as you did before. Stun him with Kneel Before Spirits and smite him with your powered-up scepter.

With Dwingvatt defeated a second time, rush east to meet the Army of Darkness once again. This time they attack from the west and northeast as they pinch down on you. Fend them off until your Orb Attack gauge and Orb Spark meter are full.

Drive her back with your stun attacks and chop her down with wide sweeps of your scepter. As Pyurrott scrambles around the field, do the same.

Dash back and forth, taking single swipes at her with your weapon. Keep dashing back and forth, striking at the Arphann

chieftain as you pass her by. Avoid her attacks while simultaneously beating her down.

OBJECTIVE
Defeat Pyurrott.

More enemies approach, this time from the southeast. Again, rush to meet them and put an end to the stream of Outlands tribes.

It's the Arphann and they bring their dragons. Even worse, Arphann chieftain Pyurrott also approaches. Let loose your Orb Spark attack and rid yourself of the

Arphann dragons. This leaves only Pyurrott to contend with.

Pyurrott, chieftain of the Arphann, kneels before you a defeated leader. Just then Syumerrt arrives. Your efforts have been successful, it seems, as Dwykfarrio has been defeated.

Before you get the chance to celebrate, Pyurrott tells you that though Dwykfarrio has

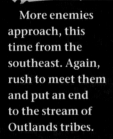

been defeated, the King of Nights' plans may still be in motion. His plan rests on Inphyy's shoulders. Suddenly, a dark ominous swirl of black and evil opens up above the flatlands. This is not over....

VIGKVAGK'S VOYAGE

Age:
Unknown
Class:
Wood Dweller
Weapon:
None
Orb Spark:
Earth

VigkVagk is a gentle Troll who, at one time, lived peacefully in the forest with other animals. But he has been captured by Orcs and, despite his innocent nature, trained as a weapon of war.

After VigkVagk was captured by Orcs, a Goblin, Dwinkle, named him and won his trust. Though his pure heart weeps, VigkVagk hopes laying waste to everything will end the war and spare his friend.

VITAL STATISTICS

Category	Level 1	Level 2	Level 3	Level 4	Level 5	Level 6	Level 7	Level 8	Level 9
Default Attack Point	100	110	121	133	146	161	177	195	214
Default HP	700	840	1,092	1,422	1,836	2,268	2,896	4,244	6,000
Default Defense Point	20	22	24	27	29	32	35	39	43
Default Rate of Critical Hit	10	11	12	13	14	15	16	17	18

COMBO ATTACKS

It's difficult to damage VigkVagk unless his belly is exposed. While playing as VigkVagk, go crazy and have fun. Always try to grab something or someone to use as a weapon to attack enemies. Boss battles will be a lot easier if you locate a nearby log and use that.

Level 1

VigkVagk's level 1 moves are very basic. Although players start off with a manageable arsenal of combos, his later moves incorporate more attacks that can be linked in chains.

> When doing a combo attack, execute button presses separated by commas in quick succession.
> If the move says ", then" or ", press", allow the final move to finish before pressing the next button command.

Move	Execution
RARR!!	ⓛⓣ
URRRGH!!!	ⓧ,ⓧ,ⓧ,ⓧ,ⓧ
Urgh?	ⓧ,ⓨ
Urgh!!	ⓧ,ⓧ,ⓨ
YARGH!!!	During Orb Attack, press ⓧ
YAARGH!!!	During Orb Attack, press ⓨ

Level 2

Because VigkVagk stops learning new moves at level 5, level 2 serves as a halfway point in his learning curve. Here he acquires a multitude of awesome moves that revolve around using people or trees as weapons.

Move	Execution
URGH!!	ⓧ,ⓧ,ⓧ,ⓨ
%$#@	While carrying stick, press ⓛⓣ
Aaagh	While grabbing person, press ⓧ,ⓧ,ⓧ
Aaargh	While carrying stick, walk or run
Agh	While grabbing person, walk or run
Buh	While grabbing person, press ⓨ
Dogh	While carrying stick, jump, then press ⓨ
GARGH!!	While carrying stick, jump
Graah!	While carrying stick, press ⓨ
Grr	Press ⓨ to pick up a stick
GRR!	While carrying stick, jump, then press ⓧ
Urgh	Press ⓨ to grab a person
Yaargh	While carrying stick, press ⓧ,ⓧ,ⓧ

Level 3

At level 3 VigkVagk learns that he can use rocks as weapons as well. Pick Up is a great move that should be utilized whenever things get stone tough.

Move	Execution
%$#@	While carrying rock, press ⓛⓣ
Argh-agh	While carrying rock, press ⓧ,ⓧ,ⓧ
Arrgh	While carrying rock, press ⓨ
GRAH!	While carrying rock, press ⓧ
Pick Up	Press ⓨ to pick up a rock
Raargh	While carrying rock, walk or run
Urrrgh!?	ⓧ,ⓧ,ⓧ,ⓧ,ⓨ

Level 4

Since VigkVagk is nearly done mastering his attacks at level 4, he learns more moves that utilize people and objects as weapons. The moves below are very effective when used on bosses.

Move	Execution
%$#@	While carrying log, press ⓛⓣ
Aargh	While carrying log, walk or run
Dodosko	While grabbing person, walk or run
Dodoskoskosko	While carrying a person in each hand, press ⓧ,ⓧ,ⓧ,ⓧ,ⓧ
Grah!	While carrying a person in each hand, press ⓨ
Grrrr	While grabbing person, press ⓐ
Nnnngh	While carrying log, hold ⓧ+ⓨ
Nrgh	Press ⓨ to pick up a log
Oogh	While carrying log, press ⓧ,ⓧ
Urrgh	While carrying log, press ⓨ
Yaargh	While carrying log, press ⓧ

Level 5

Level 5 introduces one of VigkVagk's few barehanded combos, GRAAARGH!!!. Although it drains your Orb Attack gauge, it causes massive damage as VigkVagk adds a sonic-boom scream and side slams to his fist pounding.

Move	Execution
GRAAARGH!!!	ⓧ,ⓧ,ⓧ,ⓧ,ⓧ,ⓐ (drains Orb Attack gauge)

WEAPONS

VigkVagk's superior strength precludes a need for weapons. He is a powerful beast capable of causing damage with his bare hands. Occasionally, though, he will pick up and use a tree trunk, a rock, or a Human to pound enemies into oblivion.

◈ FREEDOM...FRIEND...WARFARE ◈

VigkVagk was a happy, gentle giant living in the woods until one day, as he sat against a tree with his woodland realm friends, Orcs came with their nets and hammers. Before the Troll could react, he was ensnared in the Orcs' netting and taken captive.

A short time later, after he was trained by the Orcs to destroy and fight, he sat on the edge of the Varrgandd border ready to go to war. Then, a curiously friendly Goblin named Dwinkle befriended him. The two found companionship in each other and supported one another. Dwinkle named the Troll VigkVagk and treated him like a brother. The Troll had never had a name. He did now.

BASTIDE OF VARRGANDD

Treasure Chest

VigkVagk has no idea what to think or do. Captured by Orcs and brought to Varrgandd, he struggles to understand. But by his side is Dwinkle, the Goblin soldier that has befriended him and taken care of him thus far.

OBJECTIVE
Destroy the enemy attacking the catapults.

TIP

Because VigkVagk is a Troll and incapable of speaking the Human or Goblin tongue, he is not able to bark orders at troops. Therefore, he has none.

With Dwinkle by your side, stomp over to the catapults atop the hill on your right. Enemy Humans are attacking it and slowing them down. Barrel past the enemies on your way to the hill and snag a Human to use as a weapon.

Take your new fleshy weapon and sweep the area around the catapults. Smack the man into his friends and clear the area of all opposition.

NOTE

Keep your eye on the counter atop the screen. If the number of catapults reaches zero, the mission is over.

Before long Myifee tears open the castle gates and storms out with reinforcements. If he and his troops make it to the catapults, they are capable of ending the mission for you in no time.

Drop your Human rag doll and pick up a rock from behind a nearby catapult. Take the stone and crack it over Myifee's head. Don't get too fancy; just smack him repeatedly with the stone until he is defeated.

You defeat Myifee and keep the catapults safe until they crumble the castle walls. The way inside is clear; it's time to do some damage to the castle interior.

OBJECTIVE
Destroy the enemy at the North Gate.

Once you're inside, the enemies in the castle become easier to demolish. The area behind the fallen wall at the North Gate is teeming with warriors aching to get squashed.

Use your RARR!! attack to knock enemies back and leaping attacks to land squarely on a mess of Humans. Smash the enemy at the gate until you are called away to help with another little problem that arises.

OBJECTIVE
Defeat Tyurru and rescue our allies.

Enemy sorceress Tyurru joins the fight and brings her water-based attacks in support of the Human army. Storm southwest down the castle streets on your way to meet her.

VigkVagk, let's go help them!

You run across several troops in the street, but bullying past them is just as effective as stopping and eliminating them all. If you keep moving and just push past them they don't have enough time to pose a real threat.

Before reaching the end of the castle streets, turn back and use an Orb Attack on the enemies that have amassed behind you. Gather up their blue Orbs and return to searching for Tyurru.

105 Combo
105 Max Combo
546 Kills

Find Tyurru near the southwest corner of the castle and extend her the same courtesy you did Myifee. Bully her around until she is defeated.

9 Combo
193 Max Combo
737 Kills

Stomp south toward the next gate and regroup with the Goblin commander there. Your next task is to bring the monument at the center of the plaza crumbling down.

247 Combo
247 Max Combo
1263 Kills

Use an Orb Spark to clear out all the enemies inside the plaza, then get to work on the monument. Run up to the monument and attack it with downward smashes. Jump up, then press Ⓨ to land with an amazingly damaging thud.

247 Max Combo
1322 Kills

The statue comes crumbling down and your mission is a success. Dwinkle is pleased at your accomplishment and dances around you joyously. It's nice being able to make someone happy like that. Even in the midst of so much chaos.

PHOLYA FLATLANDS

Treasure Chest

After contributing to the victory at Varrgandd, VigkVagk is now on his way to an even fiercer battleground at Pholya. VigkVagk doesn't like to get hurt and he dislikes hurting others even more. But he loves making Dwinkle happy, and that is why VigkVagk fights.

OBJECTIVES
Destroy the enemy.
Defeat Myifee.

You stand on the Pholya Flatlands watching the chaos below with Dwinkle still by your side. Still feeling encouraged by the success at Varrgandd, Dwinkle leads you onto the field. This war must come to an end soon!

Trudge across the field and through the group of enemies engaged in battle. As you trample through them, Myifee returns for another round of battle.

Meet him at the center of the field and punish him as you did before. Push him back and keep him on the defensive as you chop off chunks of health. He dies again, this time for good.

With Myifee gone, turn your attention on the rest of the Humans on the field. Grab one to toss around the field, obliterating the others.

Just then, Dwykfarrio strolls onto the field barking out orders. He tells you and Dwinkle to join the other troops on the front lines. Fearing for Dwinkle's life, you follow orders and run off to wage more war.

Y–Yes... Sorry, sir. VigkVagk, come on.

On the way to the designated location you are ambushed by enemy archers. Arrows pour down from above and pepper the ground around you. Your thick skin can handle the arrows, but Dwinkle is more fragile.

You attempt to shelter him from the arrows, but a stray arrow impales him through the chest. Dwinkle is a victim of this horrible war, and everyone is to blame. You go into a blinding rage!

OBJECTIVES
Destroy the enemy.
Defeat Inphyy.

As you go berserk and destroy everyone in sight, Inphyy dashes onto the battlefield ready to meet Dwykfarrio, who approaches from the east. Everyone is an enemy now, Goblin or Human.

Ignore the armies. Let them collide into each other and take each other out. Instead, concentrate on smashing Inphyy. Beat her up, like you did her brother. She is very fast, however, so occasionally block her attacks before you resume pummeling her into submission.

OBJECTIVES
Destroy the enemy.
Defeat Aspharr.

Go back to the war and reengage the enemy. Smash through the skirmishes while pounding the enemy down. When Aspharr storms onto the field, run east to meet him.

Execute your leaping pound attack and knock him off his offensive stance. Relentlessly pursue him, pounding him with your fists until he is defeated. After you crush Aspharr the Goblin force is ordered to move to a southeast area of the flatlands. Head there with Dwinkle.

OBJECTIVE
Defeat Dwykfarrio.

Dwykfarrio finally shows up and approaches from the southwest with two Trolls and more troops. Ignore the troops and use an Orb Attack to drive the Trolls back. Push them away from Dwykfarrio, leaving him to deal with the Humans, and defeat the Trolls quickly.

After knocking out the Trolls, turn on Dwykfarrio and make him pay for starting the war that cost Dwinkle his life. Grab a nearby enemy and use him against Dwykfarrio. Pound away at him until he falls limp to the floor.

After Dwykfarrio, Inphyy, and Aspharr are all dead, the war between Light and Dark dies with them. You take Dwinkle's body back to the forest and lay it down next to you.

To keep this from happening again, you eat the Dark Orb that was in Dwykfarrio's possession and go to sleep.

Item	Name	Effect
	Aegis Charm 1	Protects bearer with mysterious power. Defense power +20 percent.
	Aegis Charm 2	Protects bearer with mysterious power. Defense power +50 percent.
	Aegis Charm 3	Protects bearer with mysterious power. Defense power +80 percent.
	Aegis Charm 4	Protects bearer with mysterious power. Defense power +80 percent. Recovers health equal to Orb gauge percent.
	Angel Wing	Invulnerable for a fixed time.
	Attack Power-up!	Attack power +80 percent for a fixed time.
	Battle Emblem	Guard max HP +50 percent. Player HP +20 percent. Orb gauge +15 percent.
	Black Gauntlet	Blood-smeared gloves from depths of hell. Wearer can use weapons one level higher. Guard attack frequency +30 percent. Guard archer accuracy +40 percent.
	Bonus XP!	Gives 1,000 bonus Experience Points.
	Clover 1	A rare four-leaf clover that brings good luck. Item drop rate +20 percent.
	Clover 2	A rare four-leaf clover that brings good luck. Item drop rate +50 percent.
	Clover 3	A rare four-leaf clover that brings good luck. Item drop rate +100 percent.
	Cursed Boots	Boots that bring pain and agony. Wearer can't dash.
	Cursed Choker	Necklace with design of two serpent gods. Attack power -50 percent.
	Cursed Shield	Saps the will to fight from its bearer. Defense power -50 percent.
	Dark Gloves	Assassin's gloves used for killing. Wearer can use weapons one level higher. Orb Attack length +20 percent. Critical rate +30 percent.

Item	Name	Effect
	Deadly Armband	Armband that boosts fighting skills. Wearer cannot block. Critical rate increases. Attack range increases. Won't consume Orbs for deadly attacks.
	Deadly Ring	Ring that reveals the enemy's weak spot. Wearer cannot block. Blue potions appear instead of red.
	Defense Power-up!	Defense power doubles for a fixed time.
	Demon Gloves	Gloves that summon the power of the Dark. Orb Attack will be activated when HP drops to 1. Can be used only once per mission.
	Dire Gloves	Gloves used in rituals. Enemy attack frequency doubles.
	Dire Helm	Cold iron mask that inhibits speech and sight. 0 percent critical rate.
	Dire Ring	Cursed ring that invites bad fortune. Wearer can't jump.
	Divine Armband	Grants wearer blessing from above. Critical damage evade.
	Divine Ring	Grants wearer blessing from above. Wearer can't jump.
	Divine Tiara	Grants wearer blessing from above. Item drop rate +30 percent. HP fully restored with blue potion.
	Dragon Knuckle	Close-combat weapon in the shape of a dragon. Critical rate increased. Guard break rate +50 percent.
	Fleet Boots 1	Handmade boots worn by a legendary thief. Dash range +20 percent.
	Fleet Boots 2	Handmade boots worn by a legendary thief. Dash range +30 percent.
	Giant Club	Old, battered club. Attack power doubles. Defense power to 0 percent.
	Giant's Bracelet 1	A bracelet of power shaped like a giant's head. Attack power +10 percent.
	Giant's Bracelet 2	A bracelet of power shaped like a giant's head. Attack power +20 percent.

Item	Name	Effect
	Giant's Bracelet 3	A bracelet of power shaped like a giant's head. Attack power +30 percent.
	Glowing Emblem	Orb gauge charge rate +15 percent. Both Orb Attack and Orb Spark gauges increase.
	Guard Attack Power-up!	Doubles Guard Attack power.
	Healing Wood	Player HP recovers over time. Guard HP recovers over time.
	Hourglass	Supernatural artifact that manipulates space and time. Orb Attack length +30 percent. Item effect time +50 percent. Item drop rate triples.
	HP Recovery!	Recovers 20 percent health.
	HP Recovery!	Recovers 50 percent health.
	HP Recovery!	Recovers 100 percent health.
	Item Drop Rate Up!	Quadruples Item drop rate.
	Knight's Emblem	Medal awarded to brave knights. Player max HP +20 percent. Guard max HP +20 percent.
	Knight's Flag	Rallies knights on the battlefield. Player Attack power +20 percent. Guard Attack power +20 percent.
	Knight's Helmet	Elaborately detailed helmet of superior quality. Invincible during charge attack.
	Life Crystal	Jewel with mysteries of life sealed within. Recovery Item drop rate increases.
	Life Globe 1	A jewel overflowing with the power of life. Max HP +40.
	Life Globe 2	A jewel overflowing with the power of life. Max HP +100.
	Life Globe 3	A jewel overflowing with the power of life. Max HP +200.
	Life Globe 4	A jewel overflowing with the power of life. Max HP +300.
	Life Globe 5	A jewel overflowing with the power of life. Max HP +450.

Item	Name	Effect
	Move Speed Increase!	Speed +30 percent for a fixed time.
	Orb Charm 1	A jewel that heightens latent abilities. Orb gauge charge speed +10 percent.
	Orb Charm 2	A jewel that heightens latent abilities. Orb gauge charge speed +20 percent.
	Orb Charm 3	A jewel that heightens latent abilities. Orb gauge charge speed +30 percent.
	Orb Gauge Increase!	Orb gauge increases 20 percent.
	Orb Gauge Increase!	Orb gauge increases 60 percent.
	Orb Value Doubled!	Doubles the acquired Orb value.
	Player and Guard Attack and Defense Power-up!	Guard attack rate +20 percent. Critical rate +50 percent. Guard block rate +20 percent.
	Rage Charm	Charm that awakens the fighting spirit within. Doubles Orb charge rate when HP is below 10 percent.
	Rage Choker	Necklace that awakens fighting spirit within. Attack power +50 percent. Orb charge rate -30 percent.
	Rage Dagger	Dagger sealed with a hero's fighting spirit. Orb Attack gauge full.
	Red Pendant	Red jewel adorned with glittering horse-shaped seal. Speed +20 percent. Guard Speed +20 percent.
	Royal Crown	Crown made of orihalcon. Attack power +50 percent for critical attacks.
	Royal Flag	Good luck flag that grants bearer goddess's protection. Attack power +20 percent. Attack range +50 percent.
	Royal Statue	Statue of a smiling goddess. Revives fallen allies. Player HP automatically restores.
	Sage's Glass	Magic magnifying glass that opens the mind's eye. Item drop rate triples when HP is below 20 percent.
	Statue Arm	Piece of a broken statue. Part of a set.
	Statue Body	Piece of a broken statue. Part of a set.

Item	Name	Effect
	Statue Head	Piece of a broken statue. Part of a set.
	Statue Leg	Piece of a broken statue. Part of a set.
	Valor Flag 1	A battle flag that inspires souls of warriors. Guard Attack power +10 percent. Guard Defense +20 percent.
	Valor Flag 2	A battle flag that inspires souls of warriors. Guard Attack power +20 percent. Guard Defense +40 percent.
	Valor Flag 3	A battle flag that inspires souls of warriors. Guard Attack power +30 percent. Guard Defense power +60 percent.
	War Gloves 1	Well-worn military gloves. Attack range +10 percent.
	War Gloves 2	Well-worn military gloves. Attack range +20 percent.
	War Gloves 3	Well-worn military gloves. Attack range +30 percent.
	Ward Cloak 1	Enchanted with Earth magic. Damage from catapult decreased. Physical damage -20 percent to player, -30 percent to guard.
	Ward Cloak 2	Enchanted with Earth magic. Damage from catapult decreased. Physical damage -25 percent to player, -50 percent to guard.
	Ward Cloak 3	Enchanted with Earth magic. Damage from catapult decreased. Physical damage -40 percent to player, -70 percent to guard.
	Wind Cloak 1	Enchanted with Wind magic. Enemy ranged attack accuracy -20 percent.
	Wind Cloak 2	Enchanted with Wind magic. Enemy ranged attack accuracy -40 percent.
	Wind Cloak 3	Enchanted with Wind magic. Enemy ranged attack accuracy -70 percent.
	Wisdom Charm 1	A charm bestowing wisdom and merit. Gain XP boost +5 percent.
	Wisdom Charm 2	A charm bestowing wisdom and merit. Gain XP boost +10 percent.
	Wisdom Charm 3	A charm bestowing wisdom and merit. Gain XP boost +20 percent.

Item	Name	Effect
	Wrath Choker	Awakens fighting spirit within. Cannot block. Attack power +150 percent. Orb charge rate +15 percent when HP is below 10 percent.

CONDITIONS

Chivalry Spirit: Automatically guards. Requires all three Knight items.

Rage Guard break rate +50 percent. Requires all three Rage items.

Royal Ward: Guard max HP doubles. Guard block rate +5 percent. Player max HP +80. Enemy critical rate -50 percent. Requires all three Royal items.

Spirits' Gift: Item drop rate +30 percent. Reverts red Orbs to blue. Requires all three Divine items.

SECRETS AND UNLOCKABLES

SECRET MISSION

After beating the game with every character and choosing the Varrvazzar path with Aspharr, go to the load screen and choose Inphyy. A new mission has made itself available on her mission map: Another World offers an additional ending, available only to those who have weathered the storm with every character.

ANOTHER WORLD

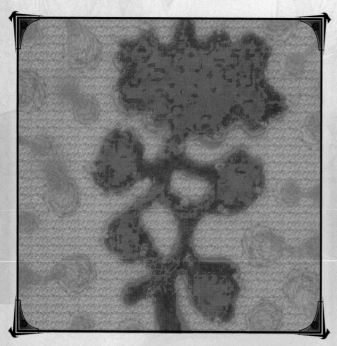

Inphyy defeated the Goblin king, Dwykfarrio, in the Forbidden Forest. But soon after she found herself in an unfamiliar place—dark, damp, and foreboding. There she meets the true enemy, the one behind it all, and faces the daunting challenge alone. Humanity's fate now rests on her young shoulders.

OBJECTIVE
Find the King of Night.

You wake up lying face down in an unfamiliar place. The air is foul and smells of sulfur. After getting to your feet, you look around to see that this is not an earthly place.

It is the underworld where the King of Night resides. It was his tainted black mist that formed around you after you defeated Dwykfarrio. That was how the King of Night brought you to this realm. You must find him. This must end!

TIP

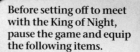

Before setting off to meet with the King of Night, pause the game and equip the following items.

- **Klausorus**
- **Knight's Emblem**
- **Fleet Boots 2**
- **Aegis Charm 4**
- **War Gloves 3**
- **Deadly Armband**

If you do not have those items, find the closest suitable replacements, such as Aegis Charm 1, 2, or 3 or War Gloves 1 or 2. Most important, however, is the Deadly Armband. Without it, you will have to rely on a limited number of minions to refill your Orb Attack gauge.

The path leading to the King of Night is surprisingly linear. Though it does have adjacent pathways leading to four large areas where battles between Outlands tribes and the Army of Darkness rage on, the main path leads straight to the king.

Should you choose to visit the four large enclosures, keep in mind that the Orbs you collect are useless for now. You can launch an Orb Attack, but you will not be able to absorb the blue Orbs they release.

CAUTION

There are no power-up items hidden in the underworld, so be careful!

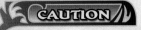

Instead of fighting every enemy on the map before reaching the King of Night, dash north, killing only enemies along the main path until you reach the king's throne room.

You arrive just in time to witness the King of Night punish Dwykfarrio for his failure while Dwingvatt stands helpless. The king then turns his attention to you. He offers you the Dark Orb, so that you may continue Dwykfarrio's journey and thus end the age of Goblins.

Suddenly, an ominous voice booms from an unseen location. It is Klarrann. He warns you not to trust the King of Night, who is only trying to seduce you. Should you trust the king, the age of Humans and Goblins will end, leaving the king to rule once again. You take heed of Klarrann's words and draw your sword.

NOTE

At the beginning of the battle with the King of Night, Klarrann grants you the power of all those that are protected by the Light. Your Orb Attack and health bars immediately fill to maximum.

TIP

An alternate approach to the fight with the King of Night is to not equip the Deadly Armband at the beginning of the fight. That way, you can block.

Instead, wait until all enemies that yield red Orbs are nearly gone, and equip the Deadly Armband before you use the last of the red Orbs on the map.

When the battle begins, ignore his minions and rush at the king. As soon as you are within range, leap over the dark army and execute Seraph Butterfly (in mid-jump, press Ⓐ,Ⓨ).

While you twirl and charge in the air, swing the camera down to aim straight at the king. Should you miss, you will land near him, vulnerable to one of his many attacks.

A direct hit on the king, if your Orb Attack gauge is full, knocks off nearly one-quarter of his life bar. Because you have the Deadly Armband equipped, Seraph Butterfly will not consume your Orb Attack gauge as long as you kill at least one enemy on the field. This is easy to accomplish.

As long as there are Army of Darkness forces on the ground, Seraph Butterfly's wake will surely kill a handful of soldiers.

After landing from your aerial attack, run away from the forces amassed on the ground, but do not kill them. Instead, simply remove yourself from the battle and collect the red Orbs you just unleashed.

Your Orb Attack gauge should remain full as long as you have the Deadly Armband equipped. Avoid the king's Laser and Vortex attacks, and stay behind him at a slight distance. If you are too close to him when you leap into the air for another Seraph Butterfly attack, you will not be able to aim yourself at him because he will be directly underneath you.

While on the ground, stay on the move. Dash around the arena to avoid taking damage. Stay ahead of his Ball of Light attack or it will knock you down, making you vulnerable to attack by his minions and chopping off nearly half of your health bar.

Watch out for his sweeping Sword Slash. He draws his sword and slashes twice. Do not stop moving after the first swipe; the second one is just as devastating. Remember, the Deadly Armband keeps you from blocking, so dashing around is your best evasive maneuver.

On occasion, attack the king with a downward slash of your sword while he is distracted by Dwingvatt. Sneak up from behind, leap into the air, and execute a heavy attack to slash downward along the king's back.

Otherwise, wait until he is about to attack Dwingvatt and continue to attack the king with Seraph Butterfly until he is defeated.

Your final blow is too much for the king. Even in his last moments, he is a vicious and bitter creature. Though he is defeated, he mutters his final words in disgust of the Human race.

Back at home, in the Divine Varrfarrinn, you meet with Ectvarr and are commended for your valiant efforts. Peace has been achieved.

XBOX LIVE ACHIEVEMENTS

Achievement	Gamerscore	Objective
Clear Inphyy	100	Complete all of Inphyy's missions.
Clear Myifee	100	Complete all of Myifee's missions.
Clear Tyurru	50	Complete all of Tyurru's missions.
Clear Aspharr	50	Complete all of Aspharr's missions.
Clear Klarrann	50	Complete all of Klarrann's missions.
Clear special mission	100	Complete the special mission.
Clear Dwingvatt	100	Complete all of Dwingvatt's missions.
Clear the mystery character	50	Complete all of the mystery character's missions.
Earn A ranking in all missions	200	Earn all A rankings in every mission of every character.
Reach the highest level	200	Build every character up to level 9.

ALL UNLOCKABLES

Character	Objective
Aspharr	Begin a profile with Inphyy and clear Fort Wyandeek.
Myifee	Clear the Pholya Flatlands with Inphyy.
Dwingvatt	Clear all of Aspharr's and Myifee's missions.
Tyurru	Clear all of Dwingvatt's missions.
Klarrann	Clear all of Dwingvatt's missions.
VigkVagk	Clear all of Tyurru's and Klarrann's missions.
Special Mission	Choose Aspharr's Varrvazzar mission and beat all missions with all characters.
True Ending	Choose Varrgandd mission with Aspharr.
Character Profiles	Clear all of a character's missions.
Artwork Library	Clear any stage.
Mission Results	Clear any stage.

THE LIBRARY'S ART GALLERY

After beating the game with particular characters, new material is added to the Artwork section of the Library. Use your acquired points to unlock each piece.

Art Piece Number	Point Value	Description
1	0	Inphyy
2	4	Myifee
3	4	Aspharr
4	7	Tyurru
5	9	Klarrann
6	8	Dwingvatt

Art Piece Number	Point Value	Description
7	8	VigkVagk
8	4	Inphyy
9	8	Arphann Warrior
10	7	Ectvarr
11	10	Inphyy and Aspharr Concept Art
12	8	Epharr
13	6	Divine Varrfarrinn
14	10	Myifee
15	14	Inphyy and Aspharr
16	11	Mercenary
17	12	Inphyy
18	5	Arphann Warrior
19	4	Pyurrott
20	4	Inphyy
21	4	Eaurvarria Mountains
22	4	Yesperratt
23	4	The Ice Gate
24	6	Inphyy and VigkVagk Concept Art
25	4	Orc Chieftain
26	6	Mylarrvaryss
27	4	Ppakk the Third
28	6	Syumerrt
29	4	Pyurrott
30	10	VigkVagk Concept Art
31	4	The Forbidden Forest
32	4	Mysterious Totems of the Forbidden Forest
33	12	Dwingvatt Concept Art
34	12	VigkVagk and Dwinkle Concept Art
35	6	Dwinkle, Dwingvatt, Dwykfarrio, and VigkVagk
36	6	Ectvarr, Inphyy, Tyurru, Yesperratt, and Epharr
37	10	Aspharr
38	15	Tyurru
39	6	Chieftain Leuu
40	6	Klarrann
41	4	King Gyagarr
42	8	Epharr
43	6	Grorgann
44	6	Heppe
45	10	Ectvarr
46	8	Dwykfarrio
47	6	Dwingvatt
48	4	Badokk
49	6	Aspharr
50	6	Myifee
51	6	Mylarrvaryss
52	6	Syumerrt
53	6	Pholya Flatlands
54	6	Fort Wyandeek
55	10	Another World
56	12	Inphyy
57	12	Myifee and Epharr
58	15	Tyurru
59	10	King of Night

RANK CONDITIONS

After completing a mission, you are given a score depending on your performance. Points are calculated according to six criteria. Add the points for all six criteria, then refer to the tables below for each character's mission qualifications.

Points Criteria

Clear time

Number of enemies killed

Number of enemies killed by Orb Spark

Max combo count

Survival percentage of ally units

Number of items obtained

Clear Time

Mission clear time points are calculated using the following equation:

Points = (3,600 – clear time)/200 + 18

NOTE

Clear time score is adjusted so that the score won't be a negative number or over 36.

Enemies Killed Points

Percentage of Enemies Killed	Points
100	40
50	20
0	0

Enemies Killed by Orb Spark

Number of Enemies Killed	Points
2,001+	26
1,000–1,999	24
900–999	22
800–899	20
700–799	18
600–699	16
500–599	14
400–499	12
300–399	10
200–299	8
100–199	6
0–99	0

Combo Count

Combo Count	Points
5,501+	20
5,001–5,500	19
4,501–5,000	18
4,001–4,500	17
3,501–4,000	16
3,001–3,500	15
2,501–3,000	14
2,001–2,500	13
1,501–2,000	12
1,001–1,500	11
501–1,000	10
201–500	9
101–200	6
1–100	3
0	0

Ally Unit Survival Rate

Percentage of Surviving Allies	Points
91–100	10
81–90	9
71–80	8
1–70	7
0	0

Items Obtained

Number of Items Obtained	Points
31+	5
30	4
20–29	3
10–19	2
5–9	1
0–4	0

MISSION RANKINGS

To acquire the highest rank in each mission, refer to the following table.

Inphyy's Missions

Mission	F Rank	D Rank	C Rank	B Rank	A Rank	S Rank	Conditions to Earn Bonus Score	Bonus Score	A Rank Reward	S Rank Reward
Divine Varrfarrinn	32	47	61	76	85	86	Kill Grorgann	10	Ward Cloak 2	Knight's Flag
Eaurvarria Mountains	39	55	71	87	98	99	Destroy the logs where Goblin archers are positioned	10	Knight's Emblem	Klausorus
Near Wyandeek	43	61	78	95	107	108	Kill the fleeing Goblins at the start, destroy buildings	20	Wind Cloak 2	Statue Body
Fort Wyandeek	28	47	66	85	97	98	Guardian's remaining HP > 20	20	War Gloves 2	Divine Tiara
Pholya Flatlands	32	46	60	74	84	85	Defeat dragons	10	Prominence	Deadly Armband
Ywa-Ue-Uar	35	51	68	84	95	96	Defeat enemy forces	10	Life Globe 2	Life Crystal
Another World	30	46	61	76	87	88	Beat mission	5	None	None

Aspharr's Missions

Mission	F Rank	D Rank	C Rank	B Rank	A Rank	S Rank	Conditions to Earn Bonus Score	Bonus Score	A Rank Reward	S Rank Reward
Divine Varrfarrinn	30	44	58	72	82	83	Find specific item box	5	Aegis Charm 2	Rage Charm
Eaurvarria Mountains	33	49	66	82	93	94	Kill the Troll before Inphyy arrives	10	Giant's Bracelet 2	Divine Tiara
Castle of Varrvazzar	30	50	70	90	103	104	The Varrvazzars' remaining HP >12 and Syumerrt's remaining HP >4	16	War Gloves 2	Bryunak
Fort Wyandeek	34	52	71	89	102	103	Guardian's remaining HP >20	20	Clover 2	Hourglass
Pholya Flatlands	40	55	69	84	94	95	Defeat dragons	10	Life Globe 2	Life Crystal
Ywa-Ue-Uar	21	38	54	70	81	82	Defeat enemy forces	5	Fleet Boots 2	Rage Choker

Myifee's Missions

Mission	F Rank	D Rank	C Rank	B Rank	A Rank	S Rank	Conditions to Earn Bonus Score	Bonus Score	A Rank Reward	S Rank Reward
Felppe Village	48	60	72	85	93	94	Rescue villagers	15	War Gloves 2	Knight's Emblem
Bastide of Varrgandd	32	49	65	82	93	94	Kill all Orcs and save all buildings	20	Wisdom Charm 2	Hourglass
Ice Gate	9	26	44	61	72	73	Badokk's remaining HP >5 and the Varrvazzars' remaining HP >15	20	Aegis Charm 2	Life Crystal
Everr Mountains	40	52	65	78	86	87	Kill all dragons	15	Valor Flag 2	Demon Gloves
Pholya Flatlands	42	55	68	81	90	91	Defend the bridge	20	Wind Cloak 2	Sage's Glass

Dwingvatt's Missions

Mission	F Rank	D Rank	C Rank	B Rank	A Rank	S Rank	Conditions to Earn Bonus Score	Bonus Score	A Rank Reward	S Rank Reward
Bastide of Varrgandd	31	51	71	91	104	105	Kill all villagers and find specific item box	20	Black Gauntlet	Divine Tiara
Ice Gate	31	49	67	85	97	98	Destroy the gatekeeper troops	20	Dark Gloves	Rage Charm
Castle of Varrvazzar	28	45	63	81	92	93	Gewg chieftain's remaining HP >5, Ppakk the Third's remaining HP >5, and Leuu's remaining HP >5	15	Rage Dagger	Deadly Armband
Pholya Flatlands	37	53	69	85	95	96	Kill all enemies	5	Deadly Ring	Hourglass

Tyurru's Missions

Mission	F Rank	D Rank	C Rank	B Rank	A Rank	S Rank	Conditions to Earn Bonus Score	Bonus Score	A Rank Reward	S Rank Reward
Bastide of Varrgandd	53	69	84	100	111	112	Destroy all catapults and defend East Gate	13	Antique Rod	Ward Cloak 3
Eaurvarria Mountains	28	47	66	84	97	98	Destroy Goblin archer logs and roll the boulder	12	Red Pendant	Divine Ring
Fort Wyandeek	35	55	74	94	107	108	Guardian's remaining HP >20	20	Orb Charm 2	Hourglass, Dire Gloves
Pholya Flatlands	36	53	71	88	100	101	Find specific item box and defeat all the Goblins in three strongholds	22	Memory Mace	Life Crystal

Klarrann's Missions

Mission	F Rank	D Rank	C Rank	B Rank	A Rank	S Rank	Conditions to Earn Bonus Score	Bonus Score	A Rank Reward	S Rank Reward
Bastide of Varrgandd	35	54	74	93	106	107	The castle lord's remaining HP >12 and rescue all villagers	22	Punishment	Life Crystal
Fort Wyandeek	41	60	78	96	109	110	Guardian's remaining HP >20	20	Wisdom Charm 2	Red Pendant
Pholya Flatlands	28	40	53	65	74	75	Kill all enemies	10	Wind Cloak 2	Hourglass

VigkVagk's Missions

Mission	F Rank	D Rank	C Rank	B Rank	A Rank	S Rank	Conditions to Earn Bonus Score	Bonus Score	A Rank Reward	S Rank Reward
Bastide of Varrgandd	35	54	73	92	104	105	Take over the enemy stronghold, destroy the catapult, and find specific item box	21	Clover 2	Hourglass
Pholya Flatlands	42	55	69	83	92	93	Defeat all of Dwykfarrio's forces	5	Giant's Bracelet 2	Life Crystal

NINETY-NINE NIGHTS CREDIT ROLL

DIRECTOR SangYoun Lee
PRODUCER T. Mizuguchi
CREATIVE DIRECTOR Henry Lee
DEVELOPMENT SUPERVISOR TaeYeun Yoo
ASSISTANT DIRECTOR TaeHoon Oh
Gilho Lee
LEAD PROGRAMMER TaeYeun Yoo
ART DIRECTOR HyoungSeob Kim
LEAD GAME DESIGNERS SangYoun Lee
Henry Lee
LEAD LEVEL DESIGNER Gilho Lee
ORIGINAL CONCEPT DESIGNER Reo Yonaga
STORY AND SCENARIO BY
Takuho Takemoto (DReSS) Reo Yonaga
Toyokazu Sakamoto (DReSS) T. Mizuguchi
SOUND DIRECTOR Takayuki Nakamura
(BRAINSTORM CO.,LTD.)
ORIGINAL THEME MUSIC BY Pinar Toprak
LEAD PRODUCTION MANAGERS Ray Nakazato
Gordon Hee
PRODUCTION MANAGERS Mineko Okamura
Tsutomu Uchida
Isao Murayama
ASSISTANT PRODUCERS Hideki Anbo
Kazuyuki Otsuki
MAIN PROGRAMMER TaeHoon Oh
PROGRAMMING TECHNICAL ADVISERS
Andrew Flavell Junya Shimoda
Takeyuki Ogura
PROGRAMMERS
JoonYoung Ahn JunYoung Kim
YongBong Choi CheongJu Na
AhnSeok Kim JaeYoung Choi
JiHo Kim BongSoo Seo
JungShic Park
ADDITIONAL PROGRAMMERS GwangSub Lim
JungHwan Ji
ART TEAM MANAGER JongHwan Lee
(RIDER-RANDY)
LEAD CHARACTER ARTIST HyunWoo Hong
ART DESIGN ADVISER Kentaro Yoshida
CHARACTER ARTISTS
YoungJune Choi HyunWoo Shim
(GPZANG) DongHun You (Elohim:WIn)
JaeKyung Uh (AURA93) HeeJeung Woo (shaorei)
SeIn Yi (sEn)
LEAD BACKGROUND ARTISTS KiWon Kim (For4d)
JongMyung Tak (Hounter)
BACKGROUND ARTISTS
YoungA Han (Kecai) Oh Han
WonHyub Kim (Leechguy) JongJhin Shin (Birdy)
HyunSoo Moon (Freecree) SeJung Kim (Flower)
Eun Young Kim
LEAD MOTION ANIMATORS JongCheul Kim (VINCAN)
YoungHyo Choi (YOCOSMOS)
MOTION ANIMATORS
JongHwan Lee EunKyoung Oh (AKAN)
(RIDER-RANDY) ByeungChan Kim (.cHaN)
YeunJea Cho (evan02) JungKyu Lee (gaepeee)
INTERFACE DESIGNER SunYoung Chung
VISUAL EFFECT DESIGNERS
Sung-Cheul Yune In-Jong Shin
Cheong-Ju Na KeyHyung Lee
Jae-Young Choi
CUTSCENE DESIGNERS HyunSoo Moon
(Freecree)
ORIGINAL BACKGROUND
CONCEPT ARTIST Toru Watanuki
LEAD CHARACTER ILLUSTRATOR JungSik Park
CHARACTER CONCEPT ARTISTS
JungSik Park Toru Watanuki
Kazunori Morisaki JeongA Jang

BACKGROUND CONCEPT
ARTISTS Toru Watanuki
JaeSeok Kim
JongMyoung Tak
2D BACKGROUND / Kensaku Fujita
OBJECTS ARTISTS Aya Hasegawa
JeongA Jang
ADDITIONAL ARTISTS
KyungHee Kim SangUn Lee
SangHyun Park EunJung Ha (hacc)
YunHee Jeung Joung Hak Lim (Clansta)
HyunSil Kim KyungNam Park (JLY)
JaKyung Jung
GAME DESIGNERS
HyungKeun Kim Masao Suganuma
Yasutake Nakayama JaeWon Shin
ACTION DESIGNERS
SangYoun Lee YoungHyo Choi
JongChul Kim HyungKeun Kim
LEVEL DESIGNERS
JaeWon Shin YangSam Oh
Kenji Yakushiji Yasutake Nakayama
YoungTae Jeong Hideki Anbo
Hiroyuki Takanabe
ADDITIONAL LEVEL DESIGNER Makoto Higashino
COMMUNICATION & SUPPORT
SoonMi Lee BoSun Jung
JungMo Koo Miho Murano
SYSTEM ENGINEERING KyoungGeun Kim
ManHee Park

QA & TEST TEAM
QUALITY ASSURANCE
MANAGER HyungKeun Kim
QUALITY ASSURANCE
HyeonSeok O SangHyun Park
YoonHo Choi DongWoo Kim
YoungJoon Cho DongHyun Kim
TEST LEADS
Masato Sasaki Robert Lamb
Koji Ota
TEST LEAD ASSISTANT Takami Kuramochi
TEST STAFF
Teppei Koike Yuji Yamagishi
Noboru Narigasawa Yoshihiro Shiraishi
Shinya Utsumi Naoki Ueda
Mitsuru Yoshikawa Yutaka Ushikubo
Kenji Akimoto Yuki Toya
Wataru Ohnuma Masateru Yaeo
Kei Setoguchi Rie Inamoto
Koji Kikawa Chika Kameya
Makoto Nakamura Shiho Takimoto
Takaaki Kirihara Akemi Sugiura
Haruki Komiyama Yosuke Fujiwara
Shizue Gotou
TEST TOOLS AND
TECHNOLOGIES Tomoko Fukui

N3 PROMOTION & GAME OPENING MOVIE
DIRECTOR Nobuaki Koga (SpFX STUDIO)
PRODUCER Hiroaki Takeuchi (Think Inc.)
SUPERVISOR T. Mizuguchi
ASSISTANT PRODUCER Misun Song (Think Inc.)
CG PRODUCER Masashi Sakamoto (Griot,Inc.)
CG ASSISTANT PRODUCER Masahiro Onda (Griot,Inc.)
ORIGINAL THEME MUSIC
MIXED BY Thanos Kazakos
U.S. POST PRODUCTION
SUPERVISION Phuuz entertainment Inc.
Ken Duer
Ken Ito
CG ANIMATION LiNDA Inc.
CG DIRECTOR Tomohiro Yonemichi
Yuetsu Murakami

PRODUCTION MANAGER Chikako Tanaka
MODELING
Akira Kawasaki Mai Nakamura
Ayumi Hayasaka Shinichiro Maeda
Hitoshi Murakami
ANIMATION
Takanori Konno Ryosuke Koga
Daichi Okajima Shigeharu Shimada
Hidemi Shimura Shinya Kouno
Hiroki Honma Tetsuya Nakano
Jitsuhisa Shibata Yasunobu Arahori
Kouji Suzuka Yuetsu Murakami
Mamoru Kushiro Yuji Sato
Masashi Fujiura
CG ANIMATION ANIMAROID Inc.
CG DIRECTOR Minoru Kusakabe
PRODUCTION MANAGER Atsuko Hashimoto
MODELING Kazuki Amenomiya
Akira Nakamura
Kiyonobu Kitada
ANIMATION
Daisuke Harada Kiyonobu Kitada
Daisuke Kazama Manabu Yoshida
Hirohisa Suzuki Ryuji Fujita
Hiroki Ebisawa Seiko Endoji
Jun Yabuki Syugo Kayano
Ji Woon Baek Takuya Imamura
Kazuma Muneto
EDITING PRODUCTION
MANAGER Masashi Kuwahara
EDITOR Yuji Ota
Hijiri Taketomi
Shunsuke Imai
ASSISTANT EDITOR Yutaka Kibukawa
CG ANIMATION AOKI Production.
CG DIRECTOR Christophe Defaye
MODELING AND ANIMATION
Anders Ehrenborg Fellah Matthias Verhasselt
Julien Weber Oliver Defaye
PRODUCTION MANAGER Makiko Aoki
U.S. POST PRODUCTION Plastic Cow Production Inc.
DIRECTOR Mickey Corcoran
POST PRODUCTION
COORDINATOR Patrick Yew
WRITTEN BY April Moskowitz
EDITED BY Evan Belfi
VISUAL EFFECTS BY Christopher Rawson
Camilo Escobar
Hugo Cabrera
MOTION CAPTURE STUDIO IBUKI Inc.
MOTION CAPTURE DIRECTOR Masahiro Miura
ANIMATION
Emi Terashima Masatoshi Kasuya
Ken Hatsuumi Takahisa Ueno
Keisuke Matsumoto Takamitsu Kousaka
Koji Hayashi
ACTOR
Colin Asanuma Inperatorisuruka
Garthe Nelson Luanna Marinho
MEMORY CAM CAMERA NAC Image Technology
Junichi Akatsu
POSTPRODUCTION AOI Studio Co.,Ltd.
SOUND EFFECT Kenji Shibasaki
SOUND MIXER Katsumi Muro
ASSISTANT SOUND MIXER Yuji Tagami

CHARACTER PROLOGUE MOVIE
SUPERVISOR SeJung Kim
DIRECTOR ChangEui Im
TEAM MANAGER ChangEui Im
ARTISTS
KeyHyung Lee SeongEun Kim
IlJin Kwon KangIl Seo
TaeBong Lim KyungHwa Hong

ADDITIONAL ARTISTS
WooJin Kim
HyunWoo Lee

NELM TEAM
ByungJoo Park — TaeWan Kim
SangBum Kim — SeoungBum Kim

REALTIME CUTSCENE MOVIES

PRODUCER — KyoungHeon Kim (I.M.C.G)
DIRECTOR / STORYBOARD — Vanz Kim (I.M.C.G / Machinema.net)

SUPERVISOR AND DIRECTOR OF ACTING — T. Mizuguchi

FACIAL ANIMATOR
Dongsun Kim — KangIl Seo
ChangEui Im — SeongEun Kim

SCENE EDITORS
SeungKyoung Jeong — TaeGyun Lee
DeokHoon Chung — ChangEui Im
Bumin Jeon — KangIl Seo
Donghwan Kim — SeongEun Kim
HakJune Lee

STORYBOARD ASSISTANT — Doucyoung Jeong
MOTION DIRECTOR / CAPTURE COORDINATOR — Shinji Takehara (Mozoo.Inc)
TECHNICAL DIRECTOR — Sakura Munakata (Mozoo.Inc)

MOTION DESIGNERS
Yoshihiro Ozawa (Mozoo.Inc) — Yoshiki Isozaki (Mozoo.Inc)
Yutaka Wakayama (Mozoo.Inc) — Kenichi Tachibana (Mozoo.Inc)
Shinjirou Nagao (Mozoo.Inc)

MOTION ACTORS
Teruaki Ogawa — Naomi Orikasa
Takako Nakamura — Ryuichiro Nishioka
Shinji Kasahara — Toshihide Matsuura
Rei Saito — Shigeru Araki

SOUND

SOUND DIRECTOR — Takayuki Nakamura (BRAINSTORM CO.,LTD.)
SOUND PRODUCTION — Takayuki Nakamura (BRAINSTORM CO.,LTD.)
Shingo Yasumoto
SOUND CREATOR — Tsubasa Waga (BRAINSTORM CO.,LTD.)

SOUND EDITOR
Syoko Ohta (BRAINSTORM CO.,LTD.) — Satoshi Ariga
Tatsuya Ikezawa (BRAINSTORM CO.,LTD.) — Yoshikazu Kamata

SOUND PROGRAMMER — Tomoyuki Hoshi
RECORDING ENGINEER — Kenji Nagashima (BRAINSTORM CO.,LTD.)

AUDIO DIRECTOR/ RECORDING ENGINEER — Yoshikazu Kamata
VOICEOVER CASTING & DIRECTION — Chris Borders
VOICEOVER RECORDING SERVICES — Technicolor Creative Services
VOICEOVER RECORDING ENGINEER — Beau Biggart (for Technicolor Creative Services)
ENGLISH SCRIPT CONSULTANT — Kazuyuki Otsuki
VOICEOVER TECHNICAL ASSISTANCE — Tom Hays (for Technicolor Creative Services)
Lydian Tone (for Technicolor Creative Services)

VOICE ACTORS
Nika Futterman — Ben Diskin — Fred Tatasciore
Amber Hood — Kim Mai Guest — John Mariano
Matt Levin — Peter Renaday — Andre Sogliuzzo
Josh Gilman — Leigh Allyn — Jim Meskimen
Cam Clarke — Baker — Michael Gough
Eric Artell — Robin Atkin — Julie Nathanson
Shanelle — Downes — Jennifer Darling
Workman — Quinton Flynn — Peter Lurie
James Horan — Leland Grant
John Farley — Stephen Stanton

Q ENTERTAINMENT ADMIN

BUSINESS DEVELOPER — Shuji Utsumi
BUSINESS MANAGER — Hirokazu Kojima
SPECIAL THANKS
Takahiko Mukouyama — Saeko Takaoka
anima inc. — Nobuhiko Shimizu
Ryuichi Hattori — Seiji Nakagawa
Takeshi Hirai — Ryo Shimizu

PHANTAGRAM ADMIN

BUSINESS DEVELOPER — Seong D. Kim
SENIOR PROJECT MANAGER — Dee Lee
BUSINESS MANAGER — SoonMi Lee
Jay Eom
MiSeon Kim

SPECIAL THANKS
YongHo Yeo — SeungAee Cho
DoHwan Chung — SooKyoung Kim

MICROSOFT ADMIN

MARKETING MANAGERS — Joji Sakaguchi
Tomoaki Inoue
ACCOUNT MANAGER — Minako Kodama
ASSOCIATE ACCOUNT MANAGERS — William Nariyuki Yagi-Bacon
Sachie Kanda
BUSINESS MANAGER — Walter Kong
Takayuki Kawasaki
USER RESEARCH — Jonah Masaru Nagai
MANUAL PRINT PRODUCTION — Fumio Yanagida
SPECIAL THANKS
Jon Burns — Miho Murano
Rod Chang — Richard Newman
Norman Cheuk — Yutaka Noma
Shinji Chiba — Shigeru Okada
Edgar M Cooke — Ray Park
Mike Fischer — AJ Redmer
Kiyoteru Fujiki — Takashi Sensui
Yukio Futatsugi — Ken Shim
Youngson Han — Junya Shimoda
Yukie Ito — Malsuk Sim
Keijiro Iwase — Raja Subramoni
Kevin Keeker — Naomi Sugiyama
Shane Kim — Alfred Tan
Eiichiro Kojima — Utako Tanaka
Yuko Kusakabe — Toshiharu Tange
Hyunju Lim — Akihiro Tashiro
Yoshihiro Maruyama — Phil Teschner
Yuichi Masuya — Hiroyuki Tsunoda
Hakurou Matsuda — Kenei Unoki
Akira Matsuo — Micky Yamaguchi
Hideaki Matsuoka — Fumihiro Yamauchi
Tacey Miller — JSC Game Institute

MICROSOFT CHINA TEAM

GROUP MANAGER — Hui Zhou
SOFTWARE TEST ENGINEER — Jiangyan Yu
PROGRAM MANAGER — Rosa Ma
LOCALIZATION PROJECT MANAGER — Free Zhai (ArtMC)
SOFTWARE TEST ENGINEER — Jinrong Shi (ArtMC)
Tao Lin (ArtMC)
TRANSLATOR — Jun Zhang (ArtMC)

MICROSOFT DUBLIN TEAM

PROGRAM MANAGER — Ian Walsh
LOCALIZATION ENGINEER — Levente Vero
SOFTWARE TEST ENGINEER — Alan Davis

MICROSOFT KOREA TEAM

PROGRAM MANAGER — Jae Youn Kim
SOFTWARE TEST ENGINEER — Min Woo Lee
Il Jin Park
LOCALIZATION PROGRAM MANAGER — Whi Young Yoon

MICROSOFT REDMOND TEAM

PROGRAM MANAGER — Tacey Miller
UX EDITOR — Laura Hamilton
LOCALIZATION SPECIALIST — Kyoko Watanabe
TEST
Chris Hind — Tony Chu
Miho Horiuchi — Allyn Iwane (Excell Data Corporation)
Jeff Stephens
David Lau — Miyuki Sakata (Volt)
AUDIO LEAD — Ken Kato
PRINT — Doug Startzel (Volt)
Jeannie Voirin-Gerde

MICROSOFT TAIWAN TEAM

LOCALIZATION PROJECT MANAGER — Carole Lin
PROGRAM MANAGER — Robert Lin
SOFTWARE TEST ENGINEER — Andy Chen An Liu
Daniel Huang
Vincent Tsai